Praise for *Life of Pei*

"Pei offers an insight into the fragility of life but also conveys the strength of human nature through a candid account of her life experiences. Her United Nations-accredited Caring for Life education program in China, encapsulates a comprehensive and essential message of compassion in action, for all forms of life."—**Dr. Zhou Jin-Fong**, secretary general of the China Biodiversity Conservation and Green Development Foundation (CBCGDF) China

"An inspiring story of a life of hardship turned to one dedicated to compassion. We can all find hope from such a path."—**Leah Garcés**, CEO and president, Mercy For Animals

"An authentic life is not created *by* us, but rather *it* creates us. Through her autobiography, meet Pei Su and her powerful journey of compassion for all living beings, reaffirming the Buddhist proverb: *One moment can change a day, one day can change a life, and one life can change the world.*"—**Michael Kaufmann**, director, Sam and Myra Ross Institute at Green Chimneys, USA

"Pei is a tenacious, wise, and compassionate soul with a page-turning story to share. She has walked a valiant path and through this book, she invites us to explore with her and draw from what she has seen and experienced."—**Jo-Anne McArthur**, photojournalist, humane educator, animal rights activist, and author

"Authentic, brave, and riveting, *Life of Pei* is one woman's saga of redemption through finding her spiritual center and her life's mission: to put compassion into action for all beings. I loved this book, and although I've never met its author, her writing leads me to believe that I probably love her, too."—**Victoria Moran**, author, *Creating a Charmed Life, The Love-Powered Diet,* and *Age Like a Yogi*

"The world needs Humane Education more than ever. I am certain that it should concern not just humans, but the entire animal kingdom and the environment. I know of no one who has greater insight into its value than Pei and her invention of ACTAsia is a powerful therapeutic initiative for the world's needs."—**Terence Ryan**, emeritus professor, Osler-McGovern Centre, Green Templeton College, University of Oxford

"A wonderful book that follows the extraordinary path of Pei and an opportunity to enjoy her straightforward, inspirational, and transparent personality. Knowing her for some 25 years, her wisdom, determination, and clear-minded vision have led her through the rocky seas of man's relationship with his fellow animals. What a tremendous difference she is making!"—**Marquis Federico Spinola**, president of ACTAsia

"This is a how-to book for activists. How to persevere in the face of personal struggles and cultural barriers. How tenacity, hard work, and vision are the keys. An unusually honest and engaging account from a true warrior for justice."—**Ken Swensen**, Inside Animal Ag

"Pei and I helped to draft the new Animal Protection Law in Taiwan, at a unique time in Taiwan's history, when it was emerging economically, socially, and politically. I have always admired Pei's bravery, her open-mindedness, and her belief in the kind nature of human hearts. She is a change-maker, and her determination will carry her through, in her battle for compassion."—**Professor Jason Yeh**, National Taiwan University

LIFE OF PEI

The Battle for Compassion

MY STORY AND JOURNEY SO FAR

PEI FENG SU,

FOUNDER OF ACTASIA

Lantern Publishing & Media • Woodstock and Brooklyn, NY

2024
Lantern Publishing & Media
PO Box 1350
Woodstock, NY 12498
www.lanternpm.org

Printed in the United States of America

Library of Congress Cataloging-in-Publication Data

Names: Su, Pei Feng, 1967- author.
Title: Life of Pei : the battle for compassion : my story and journey so far / Pei Feng Su, Founder of ACTAsia.
Description: Woodstock, NY : Lantern Publishing & Media, 2024. | Includes bibliographical references and index.
Identifiers: LCCN 2023028831 (print) | LCCN 2023028832 (ebook) | ISBN 9781590567289 (paperback) | ISBN 9781590567296 (epub)
Subjects: LCSH: Su, Pei Feng, 1967- | Compassion. | Caring. | Sympathy.
Classification: LCC BF575.S9 S87 2024 (print) | LCC BF575.S9 (ebook) | DDC 177/.7—dc23/eng/20230815
LC record available at https://lccn.loc.gov/2023028831
LC ebook record available at https://lccn.loc.gov/2023028832

To all pioneers worldwide who relentlessly forge ahead
with their mission of promoting kinder and more
compassionate communities.

&

To all young people: You have the ability within you to
change the world.

Contents

Appendices

Acknowledgments

Thank you to the following individuals & organizations for their kindness and support:

Joy Leney for documenting this book and for working alongside me as we researched my background and family history.

Lantern Publishing & Media, for designing and publishing my book.

ACTAsia International Boards of Trustees, staff and volunteers, past and present.

Deepa Balaram & Nel van Amerongen, for helping me to create ACTAsia.

Brenda Young & Yue-Xin Lee, 1881 Taiwanese Professional Women's Association, for supporting Caring for Life education (CFL) in Asia.

Dr. Elaine Ong & Dr. Chris Barton, Vets for Compassion, Australia, and Professor Jason Yeh, for developing the ACTAsia Train the Trainer (TTT) Veterinary Program in China.

Dr. Siraya Chunekamrai & the World Small Animal Veterinary Association, for endorsement of the ACTAsia TTT Veterinary Program in Asian countries.

Dr. John Lau & Dawn Kotuwage, for creating the Sustainable Fashion curriculum.

Emeritus Professor Terence Ryan and Dr. Helen Winter for introducing ACTAsia to the Osler-McGovern Centre, Oxford University.

Federico Spinola & Princess Elisabeth de Croy for enabling the creation of ACTAsia.

Iso Zhang, Jessica Su, & Kiki Zhuang, for pioneering CFL in China.

Nick Leney, for designing and documenting the Caring for Life model & curriculum.

Professor William Samuels, for the Assessment and Evaluation of CFL education.

Ross & Risa, for all your sacrifices that allowed me to forge ahead with my mission and my family in Taiwan for your ongoing love and support.

Shih Chao-Hwei & Shih Hsing Guang, for teaching me the principles of Buddhism and guiding me to understand the importance of justice and compassion for all living beings.

Wu Hung, Yu Min Chen, Sarah Wu, Jian-Lin Wang, & EAST, for continuing friendship and support.

Chang Chang-Te, Life Conservationist Association Taiwan; Han Shih Lee, Lee Foundation Singapore; Ken Swensen, USA; Dan & Kim Neal USA, for their support of CFL education in schools in Asia.

Zoe Weil, for her inspiration and support to me and ACTAsia.

Foreword

Zoe Weil, Co-Founder and President, Institute for Humane Education

I grew up in New York City, in an upper-middle–class family that had married parents, two kids, and a dog. My early life looked quite different from Pei Su's. Yet our vastly different life experiences led us toward the same path. Like Pei, I was driven by a combination of anger, depression, and empathy for others during my teenage years, as well as by a search for inner peace, to find some way to ease my internal pain.

The summer I turned nineteen, I sought out a spiritual path to help me build a life that was not self-destructive and full of despair. I took free classes taught in a rented classroom at New York University by Orthodox Jews eager to help secular Jews like me discover the values and practices in Judaism. I loved what I was learning and the community that welcomed me so warmly, but no matter how much I studied and immersed myself in the rituals I was taught, I didn't believe in God. One Shabbat afternoon, at the home of one of my teachers—and after yet another instance when I could not accept his "proof" of God's existence—my teacher said to me: "It doesn't matter what you believe. It matters what you do."

I did not realize then that he had launched me on the path that would define my life and bring me the inner peace I sought. I needed to *do* something to make the world better. Across the ocean at the same time, long before she and I would meet, Pei was grounding herself in Buddhism and learning the same truth, one summed up by singer-songwriter Joan Baez who said, "Action is the antidote to despair."

Like Pei, I began my career helping animals, and like Pei, I couldn't stop there. Animal suffering is so extreme and pervasive that it could have remained both Pei's and my sole focus forever. But exploitation, abuse, and destruction are everywhere, affecting everyone along with the ecosystems that support all life. How could we address it all? How could we build a truly just, humane, and sustainable future in which all life—human and nonhuman—could thrive? What could lie at the root of every societal system? What could turn the tide of cruelty, greed, and myopia?

The answer was obvious: education, specifically humane education, fosters compassion and prepares young people to build a future that is good for everyone. Pei and I discovered this same answer across the globe from one another, and Pei went on to build the most powerful and important humane education organization in Asia. Today, I'm honored to work with ACTAsia on our mutual vision.

Pei's is a riveting story of hope born from action, and of dedication that had its roots in despair. It is an inspiring story that I hope will launch you on your own path toward building the same humane future.

Preface

Life of Pei (pronounced PAY) is a rags-to-riches story—not in the monetary sense but spiritually and mentally. It's a story of survival and determination, written to inspire others, some of whom may be feeling lost and struggling to make sense of their lives.

My father was an authoritarian man and a secret police agent in China's Kuomintang (KMT) Party, led by Chiang Kai-shek. Following defeat by Mao Zedong's Communist Party in 1949, my father fled with the KMT to the nearby island of Taiwan. Leaving a wife and children on the mainland, he married a second time in Taiwan and took a mistress who bore him four children. His mistress was my mother, and I was the youngest child, born in 1967.

Looking back on my fifty-six years of life, I see myself as two people in one body—having lived in the last century in Taiwan as a vulnerable latchkey kid and victim of sexual assault, and now living an international life as a wife, mother, and the Chief Executive Officer of ACTAsia, a humanitarian organization working in Asian countries. My harsh teenage years saw the deaths of many family members including my mother and father. My grief was so intense that I became angry and bewildered. But with whom? I didn't know, which only added to my confusion, as I often thought of jumping from the top of a tall building to end my misery. I was so close to becoming a suicide statistic.

I sought and found solace at the Buddhist College and attended for five years, intending to become a monk. In the early 1990s, Taiwan transitioned from a dictatorship to a democracy and non-governmental organizations (NGOs) began to emerge. I became a founding member of the Life Conservationist Association of Taiwan, an NGO run by two female Buddhist monks, and campaigned for changes within the justice system and for legislative protection of people, animals, and the environment.

The work was relentless and the challenges were seemingly impossible—to the extent that I reached a "burnout," both mental and physical. Given that, coupled with a broken love affair, I felt stifled and needed to escape. Such thoughts triggered my desire to travel, so at the age of twenty-eight, I left Taiwan with some trepidation, but mainly with optimism and the determination to follow a humanitarian pathway relating to the relationship between humans and animals—not from a sentimental viewpoint but in terms of justice.

Practical work experience and studies in the United States, the United Kingdom, and elsewhere in Europe taught me the meaning of animal sentience and animal welfare, leading to my employment with the global NGO World Society for the Protection of Animals (WSPA), investigating issues specific to Asia such as bear-bile farming in China, traditional Chinese medicine (TCM), the illegal wildlife trade, and zoos. Extracts from my reports, with photographic evidence, outline these unpredictable and often dangerous investigations.

These experiences and inspiration drawn from the work of eminent zoologist Dame Jane Goodall DBE led to the start of a new dawn when my long-term vision of starting an NGO became a reality. In 2006, with no start-up capital, office premises, or sponsors, only a driving passion and belief that I could somehow make compassionate changes in the world, I founded ACTAsia for Animals (later to become ACTAsia) and began to tread my new path in life with a fact-finding visit to China. This was funded by a grant of one thousand pounds from Her Serene Highness Princess Elisabeth de Croÿ, herself a lifelong humanitarian and advocate of the human–animal bond.

Today, my main focus for ACTAsia is the training and education of children, professionals, and consumers, under the umbrella term of "caring for life." I direct ACTAsia's work in schools, universities, and communities through its multi-award–winning program Caring for Life Education, now with representation in five countries. With recognition and endorsement from the United Nations for our efforts in promoting the Sustainment Development Goals, and as the education partner in Asia of the World Small Animal Veterinary Association for our veterinary-training program, we at ACTAsia continue to develop our mission: *to promote kindness and compassion for people, animals, and the environment.*

Chapters One to Three of *Life of Pei* chart my life from a troubled child with an unconventional background to an angry and disturbed teenager struggling to make sense of life and the difficulties she encountered. The loss of family members, including my grandmother and mother, the two greatest influences on my young self, resulted in my becoming rebellious, with suicidal thoughts ever present.

Chapters Four to Six describe my search for direction as I moved through my teenage years into early adulthood. I found a spiritual family through Buddhism, and its teachings gave me a moral compass and a way of learning to accept life's challenges. Then, as I volunteered with an NGO in Taipei, I became sensitive to the many forms of injustice in this world, inflicted upon humans and animals. This work gave me a sense of purpose and self-worth.

Chapters Seven to Nine draw a parallel between my unstable early life and later journey, as I began to identify with the plight of people and animals caught up in abusive situations and became aware that abuse in its various forms is a global problem. Although my decision to travel and learn more about the world may have originally been motivated by an urge to escape from my hardships, an inner voice seemed to be ever-present, guiding me toward a different way of life.

My life and work experiences in the US and Europe were initially lonely and difficult as I grappled with the political and cultural differences between the East and the West—differences exacerbated by a disastrous marriage.

Chapters Ten to Twelve give an overview of my work with the World Society for the Protection of Animals (WSPA) as an undercover investigator and outline the potential risks of covert investigations. After five years at WSPA, I decided to resign and start my own NGO, an idea I had been nursing for many years. It was initially registered as ACTAsia for Animals, with a focus on the interrelationship between people and animals. For the first five years, with little funding available, I kept debating if I could continue. Just as I reached crisis point and had to decide whether to persevere or give up on my mission, my faith was rewarded when the first sponsor agreed to fund Caring for Life education in primary schools in China. A six-year curriculum was created and the work began in earnest. By its tenth anniversary, ACTAsia was able to celebrate with a high-profile event at the Palace of Westminster in London.

Chapters Thirteen to Fifteen describe how ACTAsia has now earned international recognition and acclaim for its training and education programs, including from the United Nations Economic and Social Council (ECOSOC) and the World Small Animal Veterinary Association (WSAVA), as well as how the Caring for Life Education program promotes compassion and respect among children, veterinarians, social workers, and consumers. In addition, Chapter Fourteen describes how my Buddhist studies and my love for music and nature have sustained me during some dark periods.

At the onset of the COVID-19 pandemic and the long lockdown that followed, I introduced the One Health approach to ACTAsia's work to complement existing programs, this being a strategy that focuses on environmental issues, their causes, such as zoonosis, deforestation, agriculture, climate change, and intensive farming systems, and their implications for humans and animals.

Chapter Sixteen, the final chapter, titled "On Reflection," follows a question-and-answer format with which I attempt to objectively analyze my former self, my attitudes, behaviors, perceptions, and actions, and how I view life now. It provides an insight into my spiritual and practical development during the past forty years.

From a depressed, lost, and angry teenager to the Chief Executive Officer of an acclaimed international charity recognized by the United Nations, I have now found my vocation and my place in life. I'm finally working toward achieving inner peace after a lifelong struggle, not least of all thanks to my becoming a mother at the age of forty, which enabled me to see life through a different, clearer lens and opened up a new world of tolerance, forgiveness, and unconditional love for me.

I now understand that life in all its forms is a precious gift, and I've gradually come to accept my early years, strewn with intense sadness and disappointment. I have taken on as my mantra this saying: *I can't change where I've come from, but I can create a compassionate pathway into the future.*

Although I have traveled extensively and experienced life in many other countries, my heart remains in Asia, and I intend to one day return to my roots and continue my humanitarian mission in my retirement.

Chapter 1

Introduction to a New Kind of Love

Most of us will remember the first time we fell in love, and I am no exception. But as this story goes, the kind of first love I was about to experience was a different one.

I was in my early forties when it happened. I was happily married to Ross; at the time, we were living in the UK, in an affluent area in leafy suburbia, with Risa, our energetic young daughter. I was happy with my life.

Then, by chance, I met him. He was homeless at the time and staying with one of my neighbors. I was curious about his life before he became homeless, but as my neighbor told me his family had died, I was reluctant to ask too many questions. He intrigued me, and I found myself making excuses to pop around to my neighbor's house just to get a glimpse of him, as he was usually in the garden.

One day, my neighbor said to me, "It's time he found a permanent home, do you know of anyone who would take him in?" I caught my breath as I heard a voice in my head suggesting, *Perhaps he could stay with us?* But would Ross agree? I wasn't sure and needed to discuss the situation with him: he might not want an addition to our family, especially as he suffered hay fever and other allergies.

As I had feared, when I brought up the subject of introducing a cat into our family, Ross remembered his childhood days when he was constantly sneezing, his eyes watering, whenever he was near the family cats. He was not too keen but reluctantly gave in to the pleadings of Risa and me. A few days later, we welcomed our new companion into our home, and my life was never the same again.

My new "beau," an ordinary yet handsome black-and-white cat of about two years old, was named Socks, an apt name due to his four white feet. His elderly owner had died some two years earlier and he was left in her garden to fend for himself, occasionally being given scraps of food by the family living next door. He learned to be a good hunter and found enough to eat, but eventually, he was taken into care by Cats Protection and placed in temporary accommodation in my neighbor's garden cattery until a permanent home could be found. Understandably, Ross kept his distance from Socks, not wanting the symptoms of his childhood allergy to flare up again. So the responsibility of caring for Socks was mine, and within the space of just a couple of months, we became devoted to each other.

I was apprehensive about how to care for Socks. As a child, growing up in Taiwan, I knew nothing about having a companion animal in the household. People of my family's status did not have the money or the space in their apartments or yards to accommodate animals, nor did they have any desire to, so at that time, companion animals were not a common part of family life. But Ross was raised in the countryside of the UK, where he and his siblings enjoyed the companionship of a variety of animals, those who lived in their house and the various mini beasts who sometimes invaded his eccentric father's workshop, so he was at ease with our new housemate and showed me how to feed and brush Socks.

For me, every day was an adventure as my love affair with Socks gradually developed into a life-changing experience. At first, I was apprehensive about touching him. I asked myself many questions: How gently should I stroke his warm, glossy black fur? Would he prefer a soft touch or a firmer touch? If I let him outside our house, would he stray onto the road and cause an accident or become injured himself, or even

2014. Socks helping Risa with her homework.

die? I was concerned when he miaowed, thinking he might be in pain, but Ross assured me that it was Socks' way of communicating with us and that I would eventually get what he was telling me. Somehow, Socks seemed to know I was a novice where cats were concerned, and he tolerated my clumsy initial attempts at showing him affection. Whenever he had had enough of repeatedly being stroked and caressed by me, he would slowly get up and move away.

I could identify with his past life experiences. The person who had cared for him had died, leaving him to fend for himself. He had learned to hunt and become self-sufficient; he was not intimidated by other cats and dogs and could stand up for himself. We were indeed soulmates. If animals experienced feelings and emotions the way I did, I wondered, was this why he had become so tough and resilient?

His intelligence amazed me. He could tell the time: time for food, time for bed, time for Risa to go to school (he would stroll along beside her), and time for her to return (at 3:15 p.m., he would wander down the lane, wait for her at the main road, then escort her back along the lane to our home). He taught me how to communicate with him—to read his signs and sounds, so that I knew when he wanted to play, to be caressed, or to be left alone. I learned that if he suddenly turned sideways and stared hard at me, he wanted me to stop fussing with him. If I ignored the signs, he would give me a swift smack and silently communicate to me, "Enough, leave me alone."

Whenever I returned home in our car, Socks would suddenly appear, having recognized the sound of the car engine, and meow in greeting. Yet, at other times, he was not so vocal; for example, when he was hungry, he would patiently sit in front of his food bowl until one of us noticed him. I called him a proper English gentleman!

At times, he demanded attention and would keep nudging me, gently headbutting my legs; at other times, he wanted to be on his own and would silently sidle into another room. When I was working at the computer, a favorite position of his was seated in my lap and straddled across my arms, such that it was almost impossible for me to use the keyboard. I often found myself apologizing to him when I had to move him from his comfortable position. His companionship was always a great comfort to me in the years of working alone at my computer that could have left me feeling isolated.

He knew when it was time for Risa to go to bed; he would lie beside her, snuggled into her cozy duvet, and even seem to listen to bedtime stories of her imaginary friends, Alice and Jonathan. Later at night, when she was sleeping, he would go for his evening stroll into the nearby woods.

2015. Pei & Ross.

This gentle, trusting cat taught me so much about the meaning of animal sentience and unconditional respect for another species.

I was beginning to understand why in Western countries, a "pet" is referred to as a companion animal. This term would have been unknown to me in Taiwan, but it certainly suited Socks. He was truly my companion, who, after he'd had his breakfast in the early mornings and Ross had gone to work in London, would come to my bedroom and cuddle up to me, his now-familiar musky smell and soft, warm furry body feeling to me like a welcome hot water bottle.

Probably none of what I'm recounting about Socks will surprise you if you live in a country where a companion animal is often described as a member of the family. But as a child, born and raised in a Taiwan that was under a restrictive military dictatorship, I never heard such anecdotes, although when I was in my teens, I do recall that Sarah Wu, one of my classmates, had a Pomeranian dog. I thought it was so odd that her dog lived inside her house. Surely, dogs were meant to live outside. But as I considered Sarah's family to be wealthy and different from mine—her father ran his own construction company and her mother worked for an American family—I assumed they were just influenced by the American way of life, which included pampering small dogs.

I was mystified to see Sarah's family was incredibly upset when their dog died. I couldn't understand why Sarah was inconsolable and cried for months, and I rarely mentioned her dog as she would immediately become distraught. I thought she was just being a "princess" who had lost her favorite toy. Other than Sarah's affection for her dog, any sort of sentiment like that toward an animal, whether verbal or in action, was unknown to me in my childhood, and terminologies such as "animal sentience" and "animal welfare" simply didn't exist in our language.

It was not surprising that any show of affection or empathy toward animals was simply foreign to us also because most parents did not openly demonstrate love toward their children. This parental emotional reserve, still common in many parts of Asia, tends to inhibit children from developing social and emotional intelligence, yet by doing so, they are more likely to grow into caring and empathetic, responsible adults. And so the cycle of indifference continues. I was never taught this at home or at school.

Most Asian parents focus on providing material support, working hard to provide their children with tangible things such as a home, food, a dowry, money for an education, even overseas studies, or for keeping up with the latest fashion trends. But while they are so busy trying to fulfill all material wants and needs, parents often miss out on building a more meaningful relationship with their children.

In Taiwan, I was taught to have respect for my elders and for authority, to be polite, and to have good manners. But none of these teachings included any reference to acts of affection. I cannot recall one occasion when either one of my parents or my grandma said "I love you" to me, but as I never heard anyone else say those words, either in real life or in books and on the radio, it did not seem odd to me. Looking back on my childhood days, I know that my mother did love me and my siblings but that she knew how to show this only through her cooking, always preparing meals with raw ingredients for us as she thought they were more nutritious than packet food. I can easily conjure up in my mind the intense heat and the sweet smell from her food cooking—usually a mix of soy sauce, garlic, and noodles. I can still hear the clanking of pots and pans as I approached our third-floor apartment on my way back from school. When Mother saw me, she would welcome me home and urge me to eat up while the food was hot and tasty, but never do I remember her asking me about my days at school, what lessons I enjoyed or found difficult, or if I had any friends or favorite teachers. Her way of showing me affection was to provide food.

In my experience and opinion, Asians tend to be more respectful of their elders compared to Westerners. This may seem to be a sweeping statement, but in many Asian countries, people are reared on the Confucian philosophical principle of filial piety, which promotes respect for their parents and ancestors. One should demonstrate this respect in all stages of their life by taking care of their parents, which is referred to as a service to the parents.

From generation to generation, schools, parents, and society in general continuously remind children about the importance of filial piety, a most important concept in Asian countries such as China, Japan, and South Korea. Asian parents have high expectations of their children and make sacrifices such as having several jobs, saving hard, and living a simple lifestyle to ensure their children have a good education and the best opportunities available. In return, those children feel a strong obligation to repay their parents' devotion and sacrifice with good academic performance, as this is regarded as one of the best forms of filial piety. So once children become adults, a sense of duty dictates that they are expected to assume responsibility for taking care of their elderly parents. But in recent years, perhaps due to global influences providing individuals with more choices, this responsibility is often seen as a burden, not something done out of love. This is not surprising. As children rarely experience love and empathy during childhood, it is unlikely that they will be able to demonstrate love and empathy toward their elders later on in life. In my earlier years, as I myself struggled with the doctrine of filial piety, I thought it was selfish to have a child just so someone would take care of me in my old age; I decided then that I would not have any children. Thankfully, I came to understand and experience unconditional love and, in my midlife, became a mother.

1994. Life Conservationist Association of Taiwan. Founders, employees, and volunteers. Pei: Row 2. 4th from left.

Likewise, in much of Asia, rarely is it suggested to children that they should behave kindly and respectfully toward animals or acknowledge that animals have feelings. Because of this, today, many children grow up still believing that animals exist just to serve humans, to feed, entertain, and clothe us—that they are no more than useful moving objects, which is what the Chinese word for "animal" literally translates to.

The year 1987 marked the end of martial law in Taiwan: media restrictions were lifted, freedom of speech and travel abroad were now permitted. In 1989, Taiwan became a democracy, with political parties and non-governmental organizations (NGOs) starting to emerge. By then, I was in my early twenties and had experienced several bereavements in my family. I was desperately searching for peace of mind and a sense of purpose in life, so I decided to devote my life to Buddhism and charitable work. I became a trainee monk and a founding member of the Life Conservationist Association (LCA), an environmental NGO newly established by my Buddhist teacher, a female monk known as *Shih* Chao Hui.

Another member of the new group was *Shih* Wu Hung, a monk at the time, who later founded Environment and Animal Society of Taiwan (EAST). He became my mentor and spiritual teacher, and together, we became activists for environmental, human, and animal rights. We developed a strong bond, and he helped me learn how to navigate the daily challenges of grassroots activism, such as facing ridicule from the public and some government departments, those skeptical that an NGO could have any power or influence in the new Taiwan.

My mentor Wu Hung and I followed *Shih* Chao Hui as she was the first female monk in Taiwan to call for Buddhists to practice Buddhism through social development, not just in the temples. She bravely challenged the media, academics, and authorities on social injustices, issues involving the more vulnerable and weaker members of society who had no voice. She was the first monk to appeal to Buddhists to extend their compassion to nonhuman animals, reminding them of Buddha's key teaching, among others, that all lives are equal. Following her lead as well as working independently, Wu Hung and I contacted like-minded people in many different countries. We attended international conferences and started to develop a more holistic perspective on animals and society.

But despite all of this, I still had conflicting emotions: my drive and enthusiasm were accompanied by periods of self-doubt, confusion, and inadequacy. After five years, I decided it was time to travel and get a glimpse of life in different countries to satisfy my growing interest in other cultures, animal welfare, and the human–animal bond. Many people helped me along the way during my travels, inviting me into their homes and sharing their own experiences and knowledge with me.

Through my experience interning and working in animal centers in Europe and the US, and also through undercover investigations and studies in sociology, I became even more eager to learn as much as I could about the interrelationship between humans and animals. I became more aware of both the numerous issues affecting the lives of humans and the cruelty and abuse animals were exposed to, even in countries where concern for animal welfare was part of the culture and had been for many decades. But due to a combination of political, economic, and social factors, not least of all indifference and ignorance, poor welfare and lack of concern for humans and animals alike appeared to be, to varying degrees, a problem throughout the world.

I have written this book for people of all cultures and all ages. At the time of writing, we are approaching 2024 and facing diverse challenges including climate change, the after-effects of the COVID-19 pandemic, the refugee crisis, terrorism, and the implications of the Russian war in Ukraine, in addition to civil wars in other countries. On a global scale, millions of people (and their animals) have been displaced, with the majority desperately seeking refuge in the US and European countries. So it is more significant than ever that we try to understand different cultures and species and to show kindness, compassion, and respect to others.

Being a native of Taiwan, which is self-ruled but considered by China to be a breakaway province, I especially understand and share the challenges faced by those who live in Asian countries whose history and tradition have not always included compassion for human and nonhuman others as an integral part. I make no excuses for any form of abuse or infliction of suffering, but I do understand from personal experience that when one is struggling to survive, living in poverty or under an oppressive regime, for example, one's main priority tends to be care for one's immediate family. Thus, it is not surprising that consideration of the plight of other people or animals is often viewed as a luxury. Those who cannot afford such luxuries tend to have little, if any, concern for animals and their habitats. At times, however, it is those who have the least who are the most willing to share with others. Compassion does not discriminate.

In 2006, with a former colleague, I set up the charity ACTAsia with the mission to educate children, consumers, and professionals in Asian societies to promote kindness to and compassion for people, animals, and the environment. Now, eighteen years later, our team includes representatives in Australia, China, the Netherlands, the UK, and the US. Some work for ACTAsia full-time or part-time, and others are either trustees or volunteer expert advisors, who willingly help us when called upon to lend their specific expertise and guidance. Education is key in everything we do, as evident through ACTAsia's award-winning Caring for Life Education programs. Lessons with interactive learning are specifically tailored for schools, universities, and communities, with practical training for veterinarians, teachers, and social workers.

I am thankful for all who have helped and guided me during the past twenty-five–plus years, for my teachers from my formal studies, as well as friends, advisors, and colleagues at Life Conservationist Association Taiwan and the World Society for the Protection of Animals, my places of work during the 1990s—and for Socks, one of my most memorable teachers. Throughout the years we were together, through our daily interactions, he taught me the meaning of animal sentience—he gave me an insight into and demonstrated for me the value of the wonderful gift of the human–animal bond.

Socks is no longer with us. Many tears were shed at his passing, and Ross, Risa, and I were overcome with grief. We were with him for his last few precious minutes on Earth as he lay on the veterinarian's table. I remember the vet explaining that Socks was now unable to breathe unaided, that the kindest thing we could do for him was to say our goodbyes and humanely end his suffering. I cried so hard when the vet said, gently, that there was nothing he could do; I still begged him to find a way to keep Socks alive. After a few minutes of my uncontrollable sobbing, Ross told me it was time to let go. Socks had suffered for a short while with an incurable disease and now looked just a shadow of our loving, devoted companion in his glory days. I suddenly remembered the intense sadness of my friend Sarah when her beloved dog had died so many years before; I could now relate to her pain. I also recalled how insensitive I had been, through my unconscious ignorance, to her loss.

As we said our goodbyes to Socks, I gave thanks for his life. His influence on me and all the practical lessons he taught me during the years he lived with us brought to life all the theory I had learned from textbooks. Being the true friend and companion he was, he provided much-needed comfort when I was going through the high and low points of setting up ACTAsia. It was as if he were cheering me on, "You can do it, it's going to work out fine." I can still feel his

1985. Sarah and Pei aged 18.

warm, silky body pressing against my frame as I sit on the chair in front of my computer. In many ways, Socks' life mirrored mine; we had a unique connection as we both had to fight for survival when the people we depended on suddenly died and disappeared from our lives. Socks taught me so much about life and love and will always have a special place in my heart.

Is it anthropomorphic to make such comments? Perhaps some readers will think it is. But he was, without question, a much-loved member of our family, and we valued him and respected him as a member of a different species with specific needs. It had taken me until I was middle-aged to fully understand animal sentience and the human–animal bond, and it was all thanks to my teacher, a little cat called Socks.

This is not a book about cats but one about unconditional love and respect for our families, other humans, all other species, and the environment. To the little Asian island girl who was the product of a harsh political regime, life has given some hard knocks, but that girl eventually entered into a world of wonderment and awe by learning about the beauty of nature and the intelligence of other beings. Likewise, we can all play a part in helping to create a more compassionate world.

I feel it is my destiny to pass on the life lessons I have accumulated for the past fifty-six years. My experiences have shaped me, and now, through the work of ACTAsia, I try to inspire others to become a part of a growing global movement centered on the simple principle that friendship, kindness, and respect for all underpin the true meaning of life. I have long realized that the work we do at ACTAsia is not just a job but embodies a belief system, one that provides a springboard to recognizing education as the key to a better world.

During the past eighteen years of ACTAsia's existence, there have been many times when the work seemed impossible, with never enough budget and people to do what was needed, and I often questioned whether I was being idealistic or stubborn, or perhaps both. Then, out of the blue, something would happen in our favor, or someone would offer to help or say something to motivate me to carry on.

The meaning of life, if one were to consult different philosophies, can appear complex and contradictory. I prefer to use this philosophical definition, which is simplistic, easy to understand and to put into practice: The meaning of life is what you choose it to be. It is not somewhere out there but right between our ears. This makes us the lords of creation.

Chapter 2

FAMILY BACKGROUND: THE PATH TO TAIWAN

I am an island girl. I come from Taiwan, a place that Westerners sometimes confuse with Thailand as the names sound similar. But although both countries are in Asia, they are approximately 2,000 miles apart, with different cultures and histories. Taiwan is not internationally recognized as a country, being legally part of the People's Republic of China, but it has its own democratic government, political parties, education system, and national health service.

I don't intend to detail the complex history of Taiwan but will give a brief overview of its people's background and how they have been influenced by different cultures. I am a product of Taiwan. My early life was shaped by a mix of many cultures in Europe and Asia as several countries have invaded and colonized Taiwan during the last five hundred years, the greatest influences being from China and Japan.

The island of Taiwan is located approximately one hundred miles off the coast of southeast China. Its history dates back more than five thousand years to the time when only Taiwanese aboriginals occupied the island, whose origins and languages were similar to those of people from the Philippines and other Polynesian ethnic groups. The island has been known by various names, including, in its early history, Tayouan. Today, like many indigenous populations around the world, the Taiwanese aboriginal population is slowly dying out; aboriginals now make up just 2 percent of the Taiwanese population, with sixteen named tribes recognized by the Taiwanese government. Out of the original twenty-six Taiwanese aboriginal languages, only a few remain, and these are gradually being replaced by Mandarin Chinese. As various tribes are slowly being lost, so too are their cultures and languages.

There are references to Taiwan in Chinese court records dating back to the third century BCE, when the Chinese Emperor sent a contingency to modern-day Taiwan to explore the land. It is also recorded that Chinese settlements existed in Taiwan before the twelfth century, with both Chinese and Japanese pirates using the island as a base for their respective operations.

But later on, around 1544, Portuguese sailors claimed to have discovered the island and named it Ilha Formosa, meaning "beautiful isle," and it became known as Formosa. But the Portuguese sailors only used the island for a few months, as a recovery base for the survivors of a shipwreck, before returning to Portugal. So when Dutch seafarers arrived, around 1624, the inhabitants on the island were mainly Taiwanese aboriginals, the indigenous people who had been living on the island largely undisturbed for thousands of years. There were also a few seafaring Spaniards living in the northern area of the island to enable Spain's trading route with the Philippines. The Dutch took over and colonized the island until China claimed it again almost four decades later.

China ruled the island from 1661 to 1895 before being defeated by Japan during the First Sino-Japanese War, so for the following fifty years, Taiwan became a colony of the Japanese Empire. When World War II was declared in 1939, Taiwanese soldiers were conscripted into the imperial Japanese military and fought for Japan, but after its defeat in 1945, Japan surrendered its colonies and Taiwan was reclaimed by China under the leadership of Chiang Kai-shek. He was a politician, a revolutionary, and a military leader who became the leader of the nationalist Kuomintang (KMT) government in 1928 after the death of its founder, Sun Yat-sen, in 1925. Upon reclaiming Taiwan, Chiang Kai-shek immediately sent administrative and military personnel to the island to establish a Chinese government and to impose order through martial law, a system of national rule whereby the military had complete control over all civilian activities.

However, at much the same time that Chiang Kai-shek reclaimed Taiwan, his power was being challenged in China. When he became the national leader of China in 1928, a civil war was already underway between his KMT Party and the Communist Party, established by Mao Zedong in 1921, but there was now a stronger upsurge. At this point, conflict had raged intermittently for close to three decades. Yet, despite the situation, Chiang Kai-shek still managed to gradually bring about the unification of China's large population, expelling communists from the KMT.

In 1946, there was a resurgence of the civil war, and in 1949, the Communist Party eventually gained complete control. Mao Zedong claimed victory and declared the country as the People's Republic of China. Chiang Kai-shek fled to Taiwan, where he already had an administration managing the island, taking with him the remnants of his former government. He claimed that the KMT was still China's legitimate government and that he, its leader in exile, would prepare to return to China. My father was one of his government officials and, as such, dutifully followed Chiang Kai-shek to Taiwan.

My father was born in 1914 in mainland China—in Nan An City, Fujian Province, a city with close historical links to Taiwan, the Philippines, Singapore, and other countries in East Asia from as early as 661 BCE. I know little of his life before he came to Taiwan, other than that he had been a secret police agent in Chiang Kai-shek's anti-communist KMT Party, with a wife and two children living on

Born 1914. Father. Born 1935. Mother.

the mainland. Recently, when researching my family history for this book, I discovered my father was trained as a secret agent by the infamous Chinese Secret Service Police, led by spymaster Dai Li.

A book on the life of Dai Li by Frederic Wakeman describes him as the most feared man in China and likens him to a "Chinese Himmler" (Himmler being one of the most powerful men in Nazi Germany and a main architect of the Holocaust). Dai Li was the chief of Chiang Kai-shek's KMT Party's secret service, a ruthless government department that sparked fear among the population in modern China. Today, fear of government intelligence agencies persists in both China and Taiwan.

After coming to Taiwan with Chiang Kai-shek at the age of thirty-five, my father was given a new identity and was from then on known as Wen Cheng. He took a Taiwanese wife, and they adopted two children. Soon after, my mother, then an unmarried young woman with a son named Chong Ren Lin, became his mistress. My mother bore my father four children, all girls: Mei Ling, born in 1959; Mei Jung, in 1962; Mei Ru, in 1965; and me, Pei Feng, in 1967. Mei Ru, soon after she was born, was given away to an uncle and his wife who were childless, so she did not live with us, but twice a year, I stayed with her and my auntie, a lovely, kind, gentle woman who endured a difficult life with her drunken husband.

I now realize the man I took to be my father had a secret life unknown to me and my siblings. But we were all young and hardly knew anything about him as he did not live with us until his later years; everything I know of him I learned from my mother. She told me he was an educated man, had studied in the Philippines, and could read and write in English. He also had a passport and was allowed to travel, which was rare in China and Taiwan at that time owing to martial law, but his role as a secret agent perhaps explained these privileges.

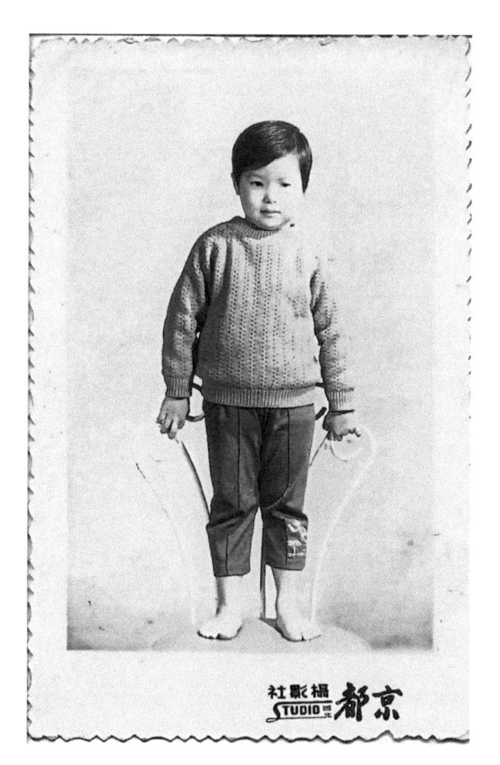

Born 1967. Pei aged 5 years.

I was born in Taichung, but we (my mother, my siblings, and I) never had a permanent home and moved frequently from one rented apartment to the next until we moved to Taipei to live with my father in 1972, when I was five years old. He had previously lived with his Taiwanese wife and children in a government house, but his wife had died two years earlier and his children were now adults and no longer living in their family home. My father still maintained contact with his other family in mainland China but had to do this secretly, because if discovered, his family members in China would be punished. I recall my mother telling us that his Chinese family was poor and struggling to grow crops to feed themselves, so on one of his missions to the Philippines, he sent them money to buy an ox to plow their land so they could grow food more easily. We knew we must never tell anyone this secret.

When my father returned from the Philippines, he brought back with him a large box of Hershey's chocolates—a great luxury—to be shared among us when it suited him. But not trusting us to leave the chocolates alone, he kept the box behind his head when he napped in the chair. One day, I could no longer resist the temptation, so when he fell asleep, I crept behind his chair and stole one of the delicious chocolates. I can picture the box now—brown, with large, embossed letters spelling out HERSHEY'S. Although I could not read English at the time, I knew the color, shape, and design of the box as it represented exotic luxury and excitement. This box of chocolates was almost like magic to me and my sisters.

I would have been severely punished if I had been caught, as my father was an austere man and showed no mercy or affection toward my mother or his children. He had a difficult relationship with my brother Chong Ren, who was not his biological child and would often challenge him. My brother always came off worst! Their strong dislike of and resentment toward each other remained a permanent sore in our family.

As children, we were all wary of our father. We saw little of him before his wife died as he was mainly with her and his other children, so to me and my siblings, he was just an occasional visitor to our home. I don't recall Mother saying he was coming to live with us, so it was almost like having another lodger—we were used to lodgers moving in and out. Even after we began living together, Father was either at work or out with friends; and in later years, he was either in the hospital or confined to his bed. We never had any fun together with him—no ball games outside or discussions about our friends or schoolwork. My mother, forever the peacemaker, did all she could to stop us from annoying him. She later told me that he always longed for a son and was disappointed that she had given him only daughters, so when I entered this world, their fourth child and yet another girl, he did not want to see me for several weeks.

Ironically, as I grew, I was the only child who resembled him in physical appearance, so eventually he became nicer to me than he was to my sisters. Because they disliked our father, my brother and sisters would retaliate by taunting me and calling me "Ugly." This became my nickname throughout my childhood, one used by even my mother, so until I was in my twenties, I always assumed that I must be ugly.

One evening, my second sister, a typical headstrong teenager quite unlike my quiet and gentle first sister, went to a dance party held at a small venue in town. She was aged fifteen. She had not asked my father if she could go, knowing he would not have given her permission, as such events were illegal under martial law. Taiwan was in the tight grip of a dictatorship: freedom of speech and freedom of the media were curtailed, and there was a curfew that banned people from being outside their homes after 8 p.m.

Unsurprisingly, the party was raided by the military police; my sister was arrested, taken to the police station, and locked in a cell. She was too scared to ask our father to come and collect her, so she stayed in the cell all night, with my parents not knowing where she was. The next morning, she was allowed to go home. I knew she would be in some sort of trouble with my father as she had openly challenged his authority. Nevertheless, I went to school as usual that day, unaware of what was about to happen at home.

When I got back from school, I found my sister collapsed, unable to move, with cuts and bruises covering her body. My father had punished her for disobeying and embarrassing him by beating her with the bamboo handle of the sweeping broom. He feared his colleagues would think he, a policeman, could not control his own daughter, so he punished her severely to make sure she would never forget just who was in control. At that time in Taiwan, it was not a crime for a parent to use corporal punishment on a child, but it *was* a crime to go to an illegal party.

When I see the love and affection Ross shows our daughter Risa, I cannot help but feel envious and wish I had known such unconditional love from my father. Unlike Risa, my siblings and I never had stories read to us, any interest shown in our schooling, family outings to look forward to, toys such as dolls or teddy bears to play with, or sleepovers with classmates at our home.

I do remember that we shared a skipping rope and played hopscotch, and I do remember going to just one birthday party, but I never had a birthday cake or birthday party of my own. Mine was a sober childhood with all the censorship of newspapers and the radio, although we did have state-controlled television and my mother on occasions allowed us to watch American basketball. One of the few highlights was Lunar New Year, a special time that we all loved as our extended family of aunts, uncles, and cousins came together to celebrate a new dawn, optimistic and hopeful for prosperity.

Our house was always busy as it was shared among five children, two parents, my maternal grandmother, and invariably a lodger

Born 1904. Grandma with first and second sister.

or lodgers to help pay the bills. My grandma and father tolerated each other but could not communicate, as she could speak only a Taiwanese dialect that was banned by the KMT and he could speak only a Taiwanese dialect that was similar to the one used in his native Fujian Province, China. The latter was the dialect my mother used, so at least my parents were able to communicate.

My grandma was distrustful of my father and never tried to hide it; she would not accept him. He was not only a foreigner in her eyes but also one from the former ruling party of mainland China, which had invaded Taiwan and imposed martial law and the curfew. She often said, in a bitter tone, that those once oppressed by Mao in mainland China had now become the oppressors in Taiwan. From a child's point of view like mine, however, it was all just normal life.

Grandma rarely spoke about her husband, other than to make an occasional snide comment about him being a useless person. What did she mean? I have no idea. He was dead long before any of us children were born and I don't recall seeing any photographs of him, so he was of no relevance to us. I do now think it unusual that my mother didn't talk about him to us, but it's often said that all families have their secrets. Mother was always mindful to keep the peace within the family, so perhaps she chose to never refer to him for fear of annoying Grandma. I will never know the answer.

In one room in our family home, we had three large pictures on three separate walls: of Dai Li, head of the secret service; Chiang Kai-shek, leader of the Kuomintang (KMT) Party in Taiwan and Sun Yat-sen, the first President of the Republic of China and the first leader of the KMT in China. He died in 1925 but was affectionately known in Taiwan as the Father of the Nation. My father remained loyal to these three men for all his life, with their pictures hanging in prominent positions in our home, as a constant reminder of his commitment to these leaders. We had four chairs in the living room, which we were supposed to take turns using, although the sitting arrangement was usually decided by who got there first and it was usual for the youngest children to sit on the floor. At mealtime, we all learned to eat quickly as food often ran out. The men and boys ate first, leaving the women and girls to compete for what was left.

My father's friends (other policemen) would often visit, and my mother said they were always talking about returning to China, but this was just wishful thinking for my father, who by now was unwell with cancer of the bladder. In 1975, when Chiang Kai-shek died, my father was distraught and knew that his hopes and dreams of following his leader back to the mainland were over. He entered a long period of mourning and his general health steadily deteriorated as the cancer progressed; he was intermittently hospitalized for treatment, which was mainly funded by the government. My mother sometimes took me with her when she visited him in the hospital, but I didn't like those visits and often would fall asleep out of boredom. Later, I would feel guilty and sorry for my father, but since we had an unusual and relatively cold father–daughter relationship, that guilt was soon overcome. Besides, I was only eight years old and easily distracted.

After an operation to remove his bladder to prevent further spread of his cancer, my father came home with a urostomy bag, a special bag fitted to his body following surgery to collect urine (which, instead of going to the bladder, flowed outside of the abdomen into the urostomy bag). In that era, the process was not as efficient compared to today: the bag was ill-fitting and there were often leakages. When my mother was at work, my sisters and I had to help change the urostomy bag, which was humiliating and frustrating for an authoritarian figure such as my father and not a pleasant task for young children. He eventually died at home in 1978 at the age of sixty-four, having existed on little more than morphine injections for several months. Although morphine was strictly controlled in Taiwan, he was able to get it through his government connections.

When he died, I was still in primary school—just eleven years old—so we only lived together for about six years, and even during those six years, we had few interactions. I don't recall ever having any significant conversations with him; I can't even remember the sound of his voice. To me, he was just someone who lived in the same house as I did for a few years. I struggle to remember his shape and size, or any of his facial features. I can rely only on the one photograph I have of him, in which he is seated in an armchair, which doesn't give me a good idea of his physique. My sisters have no clearer memories of him other than that he was stocky in stature and above average height for a Chinese man. None of us children had much contact with our father as he was very strict with us, so we learned to keep our distance. And now, even as adults, we tend to silently remember him with feelings of trepidation, not so much as a father figure but more as a lodger, and rarely do we openly speak of him.

For a widow with five children like my mother, whose main concern was how to afford the next meal, the thought of having to find the money to pay for a funeral was a huge worry. She had no spare money, just ongoing debts. Yet my father's funeral was a grand military-style affair, organized and funded by his colleagues and friends, with large crowds. He lay in an ornate open coffin so that mourners were able to pay their last respects to him; this was unusual for people other than those who were deemed to be important. The funeral was followed by forty-nine days of mourning, during which we were told to stay quietly indoors and were not allowed to go out except to go to school—when we did, we had to hurry home. Who exactly was my father? Was he a ruthless, perhaps even cruel, man? To me, he has always been a man of mystery. Perhaps my memories of him are either somewhat harsh or too generous, as I simply didn't know him. He was like a shadowy figure and was ill for the few years we lived together, so we children kept away to allow him to rest.

In his dying days, he did on occasion attempt clumsily to cuddle me, but I always pulled away, feeling uncomfortable with these unfamiliar gestures. When I think of him, the smell of morphine invades my sensory imagination and I see a man, pale and lifeless, lying on a hard metal bed. Following his death and the period of mourning, life became less strained for my family. The atmosphere in our home was lighter and more relaxed, but unbeknownst to us children, without my father's income, my mother would need to work even harder to feed us all.

Now, as an adult, I often wonder if my father regretted leaving his family in mainland China to follow Chiang Kai-shek to Taiwan, all for a political cause. I wish I had been old enough to ask him to describe his life in China and recount how Mao Zedong had managed to convince millions of people to follow communism. But as a young child, I had no understanding of the world or any other way of life. Besides, he may have gotten angry if I had questioned him, as children at that time were not generally allowed to voice opinions or ask questions, so it's unlikely that I would have been brave enough to do so.

As far as I can remember, my older sisters and brother rarely questioned him on anything, and I suspect my mother didn't either as she was accepting of her life and always tried to keep the atmosphere in our home as calm as possible. I often ask myself if my father was a heartless, uncaring person or if he was a young man with good intentions, caught up in an ideology. These questions play over and over in my mind when I reflect on the past, but I am resigned to never knowing the answers. I was never a happy or relaxed child. For as long as I can remember, my childhood was dominated by my father's illness and the endless hospital visits, which put a heavy burden on us all. It was such a relief when I was free of that burden.

Chapter 3

Maternal Influences

My mother was born in 1935 in Taidong, located in the southeastern area of Taiwan and colonized by Japan during the Sino-Japanese War of 1937–1945. She had no knowledge of her background other than that she was a twin. Both she and her twin sister had been sold to different childless families and met again as adults on only one occasion, for what reason I don't know. It was common practice at the time for unwanted children, especially girls, to be sold to childless couples or couples wanting to add to their existing families. (The "one-child policy," which was later introduced in 1979 in China, was never imposed on Taiwan.)

My mother had no formal education, as native Taiwanese were largely uneducated and those living in rural areas were treated as second-class citizens under Japanese rule. She had just six years of schooling, during which only the Japanese language was used, so she could not read, write, or speak Mandarin and had no qualifications.

My mother's name was Mang Wang, but her friends called her Chin Ye, which means "golden leaves." She was pretty, with very pale, almost translucent skin, which in Chinese culture is highly desirable. She never wore makeup other than a dash of lipstick and, most importantly for her, emphasized eyebrows, which she lined every day with a coloring pencil. I loved to watch her do this; she would often say, "Remember, eyebrows are very important as they frame your face, otherwise people won't know if they are looking at the front or the back of your head." I always thought this was a strange thing to say, but as I grew older, I understood what she meant—"make yourself noticed"—and I often find her words flitting through my mind as I apply my own makeup.

Her facial features were not typical of a Chinese woman as her nose was straighter, with just a slight curve, compared to the conventional, wider-spread nose. She was short and slight in stature—in this she was typical—with straight black hair. Every morning, after washing her face and applying her lipstick and eyebrows, she would sweep the floors of the living areas with a witch's broom, a bunch of twigs tied onto the end of a long bamboo pole. Sweeping these floors eventually became my daily chore, which had to be done every day of the year except Lunar New Year's Day. No sweeping or washing of clothes was done on this special day as it was believed that good fortune for the coming year would be swept or washed away.

When my father fell ill, the government gave him a pension; it stopped when he died. This must have been a very difficult time for my mother, with no financial assistance available from the government or any other source of funds. But although she was uneducated in a conventional sense, she was streetwise and resourceful. I remember we all slept in the same room to keep warm and simultaneously rent out other rooms to lodgers. My mother worked long hours, sometimes having three or four jobs at the same time, to make sure we had enough money for food and clothes—at one stage, she ran a bar, a laundry, and a hair salon—and also regularly borrowed from moneylenders.

I now realize what a hard life she had as she was the sole provider for seven of us, including my maternal grandmother, my mother's adoptive mother. We lived in rented apartments. When we couldn't pay the rent, we would move on to a less expensive place, or my mother would borrow from one lender, then from another to repay the former. At times, she was juggling as many as five lenders. It must have been so stressful for her, trying to keep her finances afloat, especially as Grandma was diabetic and needed costly medications.

But I think she was determined to make the best of her life. She tried to be optimistic and always welcomed friends, aunts, and uncles to our humble home with a warm smile. She took pride in her appearance: she always kept her hairstyle neat and tidy and carefully looked after her few clothes, making sure they were clean and neatly pressed. She often said to us children, "I know we are poor and have little money, but if we look clean and smart and are cheerful, people will want to visit us, and this will bring us better luck in the future."

I was brought up mainly by my grandma and became very close to her, as my mother was always busy working. As a young married woman, Grandma had given birth to two sons and adopted two baby girls, one of them my mother. Now, in her later life, she moved between her children's families, no longer having her own home. She was kind to me and gave me the attention that my mother simply had no time to provide, with most of her waking hours occupied by her relentless work schedule.

Grandma's face was wide between her cheekbones, and her hair was scraped back to form a bun sitting at the nape of her neck in the style favored by most elderly Chinese women at that time. Her back was stooped, but she could still walk at a sprightly pace, or so I thought as I was a young child at the time and didn't walk very quickly.

Grandma made my clothes and altered my sisters' clothes to fit me when they'd been outgrown. She took me shopping for food and to see her friends. She often took me with her to visit her son. There were no motorways or fast coaches in those days, so we traveled on rickety buses along bumpy and windy roads to Keelung, which was only about fifteen miles from Taipei, but the journey took more than two hours as there were so many stops for people to get on and off.

I would snuggle up to her when I was tired and although she didn't cuddle me, I remember how I would stroke her earlobe, which was so soft and warm. I had no toys, no dolls or teddy bears, so Grandma's earlobe was my source of comfort before I fell asleep. I adored her, although others in the family said she was harsh and demanding, sharp-tongued, and difficult to please. To me, she was my lovely grandma, and I liked having her around—it made me feel more secure. I missed her so much whenever it was time for her to move on and stay with one of her other children's family members, and I counted the days until her return.

One of Grandma's sons died, so she doted on her surviving son, who became a banquet chef (he and his wife adopted my third sister, Mei Ru). He was a difficult man who drank too much and, at times, behaved badly. He relied on seasonal work and lived beyond his means, so he was always scrounging for money. Grandma would cry and insist that my mother give him money. When my father was alive, situations like this would make him very cross, so my mother was secretive, even as Grandma made my mother give her son money to help him buy his house, which now seems to me such an unreasonable demand. Was it because he was her blood relative, whereas Mother was not?

One of my earliest memories is of going with my grandma to visit her auntie in Keelung when I was about four or five years old. We were greeted by an old lady who could barely shuffle along, moving in a bent-over position. She wore a long skirt, with strange-looking shoes poking out from underneath. I didn't speak with her as children were expected to be quiet when in the company of adults, so I only remember her strange shuffling movement and her small, square-shaped shoes. Although I had no idea at the time, she had bound feet. Only later did I realize, looking back on the visit as an adult and doing my research.

Foot-binding was an excruciatingly painful practice in China and Japan that, over the span of centuries, maimed millions of girls and women. When a child was about seven years old, her toes and the arches of her feet were broken and bound tightly with a cloth to the soles of her feet to produce impossibly small feet, which were thought to be a sign of beauty that would improve her chances of marrying someone of high status. On the other hand, some theories now suggest the practice may have begun for economic reasons as families depended upon girls and women for income. It was a way of making sure that young girls could not run and play, that they would just sit still and help their families make goods to sell, such as yarn, cloth, mats, shoes, and fishing nets.

The practice of foot-binding in China was banned in 1912, but since the law was not enforced, it continued in some rural areas for several decades. The image of that old lady trying to walk has stayed with me all my life and is as vivid now as it was the day I saw her. This practice, which today would be labeled as child abuse, has undoubtedly caused great suffering to generations of young girls, and I still feel so sad for that old lady, knowing she spent a lifetime being in pain and discomfort.

* * *

Although my mother showed no physical signs of affection toward any of her children, if she was working away from our hometown and Grandma was not staying with us, she would get a friend to cook for us so that we would always have a hot meal each day. I later realized just how much she loved us all, how strong her sense of duty was, and how hard she worked to keep us together. She was always so happy when she earned enough money to give us a treat. She would cook us a special meal, such as noodles mixed with pig's heart and liver, with spinach and offal as a side dish. When money was scarce, we ate pig's ears and lungs, which were chewy.

1994. One of many ornate temples in Taiwan.

Some of my best memories with my mother involved going with her to shop for food at traditional wet markets, and the very best time was when she bought me a dress from a shop, my clothes usually being my sisters' cast-offs. It was the first and last time I had a new dress until I was working and able to buy my own clothes.

I also loved going with my mother to the temple; we went once or twice a month. We celebrated the birthdays of the gods, and she would cook as much food for us as she could afford. The Month of the Ghosts was a special time: in each district, a pig who had been force-fed for several months was then slaughtered in full view of everyone in the vicinity and cut up, providing enough food for the entire district. I now find it hard to believe that I enjoyed an event during which a pig was brutally killed, but at the time, I was with my mother and my family, and we were all happy. That was all that mattered.

The Month of the Ghosts, which takes place each year from the first day of the seventh lunar month, is the time of the year when

Taiwanese believe that the gates of Hell open and restless souls spend thirty days and thirty nights in the land of the living. This is symbolized by the opening of the gates to temples so that the ghosts are free to roam the island to find food and entertainment. During this time, families offer prayers and light incense in honor of deceased relatives. The celebrations include a stage erected for Chinese opera performances, with singing and dancing.

My parents loved Chinese opera. My father, thinking I had potential as an opera singer, on one occasion arranged for me to have an audition. I was so nervous and as I tried to sing, little more than a squeaking sound came out of my mouth. He was not amused, and I was embarrassed, so my singing career was over.

Birthdays, if remembered, were some of the best days for us. There was no present or cake, but if we had money to buy eggs, the birthday person received a special red egg. This was simply a hen's egg tinted red with food coloring and, if we were especially lucky, served with chicken

1994. The outside perimeter of a temple in Taiwan.

thighs and noodles. As no one remembered the actual date of my birth, I was registered with the same date and month as was my third sister, only two years later, so we enjoyed celebrating our birthdays together.

In my mind, happy memories of my childhood are always marred by unpleasant ones. Some of those memories are of events that happened when we lived in our first home in Taipei. I was five years old. Back then, family friends would often refer to me as a chubby little girl, not pretty, but sweet and cute. In the evenings after dinner, when the family was busy, my sisters with their homework and my mother with either cleaning up or work, I would quietly go to the apartment on the top floor of our building, where a man would talk to me through the metal railings of the window, ask me to touch his private parts, and then give me sweets. He told me I must not tell anyone what we were doing, and I agreed. I was often told by my mother never to accept sweets from strangers, but I didn't think of this man as a stranger because we knew him. Also, sweets were such a rare luxury.

A similar situation happened when I was almost six years old and we had moved to another building on a street with a shop located at one end. I was now allowed to walk to the shop on my own and was often sent there by my mother to buy items such as a bottle of soy sauce or a packet of sugar. The shop owner's son always spoke kindly to me. While I stared in envy at the variety of sweets in large glass jars—I could imagine eating them all—he would wrap his arms around my shoulders, put his hands into my pants, and touch my private parts. Again, I was rewarded with sweets, and I kept silent.

Being as young as I was, I felt I was naughty for taking the sweets and dared not tell anyone what had happened. Even when I grew up, deep down, I was ashamed and felt extremely stupid and angry with myself. I never told this to anyone (until now), even my husband, the rest of my family, or my friends, despite being outspoken on so many other issues.

1997. Four sisters: Mei Ling, Mei Ru, Mei Jung, Pei Feng (Pei).

At the time of the abuse, my father was ill, my mother was working or busy with chores, and my grandma was staying in another city with her son (the adoptive father of my third sister), so no one was aware of what was happening. At that time in Taiwan, issues relating to sex were largely not spoken about, and probably only a few people were aware that pedophiles were living in their community, or even that pedophiles existed. It is well documented that sexual abuse of children has lasting effects on the victims. The offender often remains free, whereas the vulnerable child is chained by feelings of guilt that seem to increase over the years rather than diminish. I know this to be true as it applies to my own experiences.

My second sister, Mei Jung, is five years older than me. When I was six, on my first day of primary school, she was the one who made sure I was clean, tidy, and on time. I was not prepared for school: since we couldn't afford the fees, I hadn't gone to kindergarten as was the norm. In kindergarten, children are taught to recognize many words and write their names; I was unable to do these things. My teacher was sympathetic and allowed me to occasionally go to my sister's classroom for some tuition from her, and so my second sister became my second teacher. I turned eight years old before I could read and write.

Mei Jung was a very capable girl, fiery and vocally strong. I felt protected when I was with her. Whenever I was upset or confused, I would run to her for comfort. Whenever I cried—I remember always crying about one thing or another—I would count on her to sort out my problems. But as time went by and I grew older and more defiant, I became wayward and would often ignore her, even though she was usually just trying to help.

My first sister, Mei Ling, strongly resembled my mother in facial appearance, as did my brother Chong Ren. Mei Ling had the same light-colored, unblemished skin as did Mother; her paleness and open expression made her look like a delicate flower fairy. She was much quieter than my second sister, and although three years older, she relied on her younger sister to make decisions for her. When she was a small child, she ran in front of a lorry and was badly injured. My mother always said it was a miracle she'd survived, but because of her terrifying experience, she developed a nervous disposition, so I never went to her with any of my childhood problems as I didn't want to worry her. Thus, Mei Jung, though younger than Mei Ling, was like a second mother to us all.

Chong Ren was seventeen years old when we came to Taipei to live with my father. He had recently left college and was working for an export broker company. Being the firstborn and boy in a family of girls, he was the golden child. My grandma and my mother were both fiercely protective of him, and he had a room to himself in our overcrowded home while we girls all shared one room. I saw little of him as he was either at work or out with his friends and when at home, he preferred to stay in his room. He is twelve years older than me, so we also had little in common.

1979. Mother with my brother, Chong Ren.

Chong Ren and my mother had a special bond that my sisters and I resented. When he was getting married, my mother, following Taiwanese tradition, wanted to give him money to buy some gold for his bride-to-be. My sisters were unhappy about this as he was working and could use his own money. Why should Mother get into further debt? On the other hand, my father never accepted Chong Ren (as he was not my father's biological son) and vice versa. It must have been hard for my mother to try to keep the peace between her much-loved son and my father. But Chong Ren did have a staunch ally—Grandma, in whose eyes he could do no wrong and my father could do no right!

I often wonder how my mother managed to stay so cheerful when she was actually walking a tightrope, trying to be the glue that bound us all together.

Chapter 4

Surviving the Storms

I was devastated when my grandma died at the age of seventy-two. I was just nine years old. Her death left a huge gap in my life, and from that time on, my sisters and I were "latchkey kids" as Mother was always working and there was no one at home when we got back from school. Now that Grandma was no longer around to keep watch over us, my sisters and I had to fend for ourselves. The loss of my grandma was also my first encounter with death. Little did I know that the coming years of my youth would be punctuated by the deaths of so many people who were close to me.

I remember one day when I arrived home from school, I could hear lots of shouting and crying. Too scared to go into the house as I didn't recognize the voices, I waited outside for my sisters to come home. I was told later that our lodger had been attacked by her boyfriend after he had discovered she was having an affair with another man. I can't remember much else of what happened other than that they both left our home soon after the incident. Perhaps my mother asked them to leave, not wanting the police to get involved. Still, the incident unsettled me and for some time afterwards, whenever I got home from school, I would wait outside the house for my sisters to arrive before going in. How I wished my grandma were still with us!

***

My grandma's coffin was kept outside my uncle's house for forty-nine days, the duration of the traditional period of mourning. My uncle lived in Keelung, at the top of a hill too steep for a car to drive up, so the coffin was not blocking the road from any traffic.

According to the tradition at that time, a coffin had to be guarded in shifts throughout the day and night to stop any cats from jumping over it; otherwise, it was thought that the dead person would not be reincarnated in the next life and might become a vampire. Family members and close friends sat with a person who had died to show loyalty, protecting the human form of the deceased as they traveled to the afterlife. Mourners brought white flowers, and professional crying ladies were hired to mourn loudly throughout the day and night, starting and stopping abruptly. This was usual in Taiwan at the time. The louder the crying, the greater the respect shown for the deceased. It was done most dramatically and was so frightening, especially when accompanied by strange activities such as onlookers spontaneously running around the coffin to keep evil spirits away. Other rituals included offering food and (paper) money to the deceased; paper money or joss paper, designed to look like real money and made from bamboo or rice paper, was to be burned and symbolized the money that the deceased would need in the afterlife. Feng Shui, a popular tradition centered on the belief that the positioning of physical objects can affect the flow of energy (*chi*), was used to make sure the location of the dead person's grave would give good chi to their living family.

Being only nine years of age, I found the ceremonial rituals rather scary and depressing; there was nothing about death and funerals that appealed to me. Yet it seemed to me that if we didn't follow those rituals, bad things would happen, like some sort of curse. And so I convinced myself that all the rituals were important to ensure peace for the deceased in the afterlife, as well as good health and happiness for the family in the future.

c. 1953. Mother with her niece and two friends.

Death was a significant part of my prepubescent and teenage years, between the ages of nine and fifteen. During this period, not only my grandmother and father died, but so did a cousin and my aunt and uncle, the adoptive parents of my third sister. To both my sister and me, this was a tragedy. I had spent my summer holidays with them all. I had loved being with my third sister and my auntie and often wished I lived with them instead. Auntie was a simple, uncomplicated woman, and so very kind. Sadly, after she died, my uncle, devastated by her death, started to drink heavily to try to block out his misery. During one drunken spree, he fell and broke his neck. He was paralyzed and died shortly after the fall. My third sister came to live with us after the loss of her adoptive mother and father, being reunited with her biological family after having been given away as a baby. But fate determined that this would not be for long.

My mother loved to visit and seek advice from fortune tellers. Having to constantly struggle for her family's and her own survival, she searched for ways to avoid bringing more difficulties into her life, so whenever she heard of a reliable fortune teller, she and her friends would pay a visit, hoping for some exciting or happy predictions. In 1983, when my mother was forty-eight years old, she went to see a fortune teller and was told, unexpectedly, that something could happen to her that year, that she might even die, but that if she managed to get through this crisis, she would enjoy a long life. When she came home, she told us a little of what advice she had been given and said she must be cautious for the coming year not to take any risks regarding her health or safety. She did indeed follow the fortune teller's advice and would not go out unless it was essential (she had to go to work of course), fearful that she might get into an accident.

That year, my mother traveled outside of Taiwan to work as a hotel chambermaid, coming home just one day a week to see us children. For several weeks, whenever she came home, she seemed to have a persistent cough, and I could hear her coughing throughout the night as I slept in the same room. Finally, my first sister managed to persuade her to go see a doctor during her next visit, which would be the following Friday evening. When Friday came around, however, Mother protested that she did not want to go to the hospital as there was no health insurance scheme in Taiwan; as always, she was occupied with thoughts of how to fund the appointment. But my first sister was insistent, assuring her that somehow, we would find the money to pay for any necessary treatment.

After examining my mother, the doctor said that she should be admitted to the hospital immediately. This was a big shock to all of us, and I remember thinking, *Why does she need to stay in the hospital for a cough?* She ended up staying there overnight, and when we all visited her the following day, I was stunned to see her wearing an oxygen mask and connected to a machine to help her breathe. The nurse told us they were unable to run any further tests as it was the weekend and there were no senior consultants on duty, only junior doctors to deal with routine matters.

We visited again the next day, and as the five of us siblings and an auntie surrounded her bed, we were all anxious to know what was wrong with her, and nervous and worried to see her look so frail. Sensing our anxiety, she tried to rouse herself, and ever the protective mother, she smiled and told us to go home as she was feeling much better. Auntie reluctantly bustled us out of the hospital, but we were all unwilling to leave. We felt so apprehensive about leaving our mother on her own—that she might feel scared or lonely.

We said nothing to each other on the journey home. The house, upon our entering, seemed eerily quiet. It felt like a calm sea before a storm. Not wanting to have conversations, we all went to bed early that evening at around nine o'clock, willing time to speed up and the next morning to come so that Mother could have her tests done. Shortly after midnight, the phone rang, and my brother rushed to answer it. I heard his sudden scream, followed by uncontrollable wailing. We all leaped from our beds. Mother had passed away from tuberculosis.

She died in the cold winter, before Chinese New Year. She was not yet forty-nine. I was only sixteen years old, having not long left school and now studying commerce in my first year of college. Shock and bewilderment took over. I was unable to grasp that she had been taken so quickly without us realizing she was so ill, and overcome with guilt as I had slept in the same room with her all my life, including the months before she died. I had heard her coughing at intervals throughout the night, thinking she just had a cold that was more persistent than the usual ones we all caught from time to time.

We all felt so ashamed and distraught that our mother had died in a cold hospital bed, without her children around her. We had not said goodbye to her. I had not been able to give her a cuddle or stroke her beautiful, soft face for the last time. I was angry that in her last year of life, she had lived in fear due to that fortune teller. I have always thought she deserved so much more from life. I find myself crying as I recount this painful experience; the unfairness of it still feels so raw even though it was more than forty years ago.

Following the death of my mother, my brother moved back into our home. He was married by now and brought his wife, Susan Su, with him. Almost overnight, we became a group of six lost young adults—four sisters, a brother, and a sister-in-law—all fearful about the future. We were all in a state of disbelief that our mother, who, through sheer hard work and determination, had been the glue holding our family together, was no longer with us. And once again, we had to go through the funeral rituals and the long period of mourning.

We had no money, but since it was customary for friends of the deceased to give money to the immediate family, we were at least able to cover the costs of a basic funeral. At the time, people preferred burial to cremation, but Taiwan being a densely populated island, the cost of land at burial sites was way beyond our means. So Mother was cremated, and her ashes were taken to a state-run concrete tower in Taipei for safekeeping. Many years later, when all of us had become adults with income, we paid for our mother's ashes to be removed from the impersonal, ugly concrete tower and taken to her final resting place at a peaceful temple with beautiful surroundings, where my father's ashes are also placed. This temple sits on the edge of a national park, surrounded by cherry blossom trees, with views of the mountains. We all felt much happier knowing that although we as children had been unable to do much for her to ease her hardships, we were now able to give her the dignified respect she so deserved. Incidentally, in Buddhism, it is believed that burying or keeping the ashes of a loved one in a beautiful environment will bring good fortune to future generations.

1990. Family wedding of second sister, seven years after mother died.

Nevertheless, following Mother's funeral, we still had to face the many debts that we inherited from her, and it took us, my brother and my two older sisters being the main contributors, years to repay them all.

My brother tried to take on the role of head of household, and probably out of intense grief, he and his wife decided to move all of our mother's photos and trinkets from the living areas to his room. Perhaps he felt such pain whenever he saw anything that reminded him of her that he wanted to remove all visible traces of her, even her piggy bank for petty cash. My sisters and I were enraged: we wanted Mother's few possessions and pictures of her to surround us and bring us comfort, allowing us to imagine her still being here. For months on end, we bickered and argued aggressively, giving vent to our emotions and frustrations instead of trying to console and support each other.

My mother's death left my brother outwardly distraught, and the rest of us were subject to his outbursts of vitriolic abuse. The loss of the person he had always relied on to be on his side was too much for him to bear. Being my mother's eldest but not my father's biological child, he had always been protected by Mother even as Father never accepted him as family. When my mother, then a single woman, gave birth to my brother, it would have made her life much easier to sell him to a couple wanting a child, as often happened in Taiwan at the time, but her choosing to keep him proved that she always loved him and tried to care for him as best she could.

During the coming weeks and months, we all became quiet and depressed, communicating less and less and staying mainly in our bedrooms, which became our personal sanctuaries. The apartment had three bedrooms: one for my brother and his wife, one for my first and second sisters, and one for my third sister and me. Once a united family, we were now divided. I was unable to speak without crying and wore only grey clothes for one year—I'm not sure why, but at the time, it seemed a respectful thing to do. The death of my mother

Aug. 1994. The month of the Ghosts with food and offerings set out on tables.

marked the beginning of a new reality for us, one that was grey and drab as any color in my life was now gone.

Looking back, I can see how my siblings and I had broken up into separate parts of a previously solid unit. Instead of looking out for each other, we had become self-centered, consumed by our grief. In crisis mode, we seemed incapable of pulling together for mutual support. We had never been close, and now it seemed too late to try to reach out to one another.

The deaths of so many loved ones in a period of a few short years had a profound effect on my teenage thoughts, some of which were suicidal while others were less dramatic, but which always questioned life and death and searched for answers. I was convinced that I was not a good person and that this was why bad things happened to me. I was convinced that my destiny was a life full of misery and sorrow. Did I want to live out my life this way or end it right then and there? Sometimes, I imagined myself jumping off a high building and thought about how free it must be to die in this way. I realize now, of course, that it was abnormal and disturbing for a young girl to constantly have such dark thoughts and to spend many hours alone contemplating suicide.

At that time in Taiwan, there was little, if any, understanding of depression or mental health issues in general. Nonetheless, a friend of my sister's became concerned for me and, as he lived in the countryside and was used to seeing young people play with dogs and cats who roamed around, decided to give me a puppy as a distraction. Little did we know that his kind act would turn into a disastrous experience for both me and the innocent dog.

None of us had any idea how to look after a dog, nor did we even want one, but he arrived nonetheless—a nondescript, small, white puppy called Toby. By now, we had moved yet again to an apartment on the fourth floor of a high-rise building, with no outside area other than a small balcony. We left this poor puppy in a crate on the balcony from 7 a.m. to 6 p.m. each day, as I was at college and my sisters and brother were all at work. When we came home and let him out of the crate, he would urinate and mess on the floor either from excitement to see us or in desperation to relieve himself. This annoyed us and the poor dog would be punished—at best scolded, at worst smacked hard—for causing us the inconvenience of cleaning up after him.

On occasions, I did feel sorry for him. He was not keen on the rice and mince meals we were giving him, so I would use my lunch money to buy him some barbecue spiced offal, which he loved. I didn't know that there was special dog food or that the too spicy and salty offal was unsuitable food for a young dog. We never considered vaccinating him, taking him to the veterinarian, or even for a walk.

One day, I came home from college to find Toby with his hair shaved close to his skin and covered in red spots. My sister-in-law, becoming increasingly anxious, had taken him to the veterinary clinic, where he had had multiple ticks removed. We were all horrified that the house might become infested and we ourselves might get bitten. My sister-in-law insisted we should part with him as we were incapable of looking after him and, in any case, none of us really wanted him. No one objected, so Toby was returned to my sister's friend in the countryside. I was relieved to see him go, though possibly a little disappointed. It certainly turned out to be the best decision considering how much harm our indifferent behavior was causing to the little puppy, as I later learned.

Feelings of shame and sadness sweep over me now as I relive our time with Toby; I am ashamed and saddened that I was so oblivious to the needs of a helpless living creature. We were too ignorant and absorbed with our grief, too self-obsessed and indifferent to consider Toby's well-being. We had no awareness or understanding of animal sentience and welfare. Painful personal experiences had numbed my senses and emotions, pushing me into a downward spiral of callous behavior, devoid of compassion.

Not long before Mother died, she brought home two duvet covers with Mickey Mouse designs. It was an amazing day. We were never able to afford new, let alone branded, goods; these duvet covers were therefore an extreme luxury. She had been saving to get us something special, but her money could stretch to only two covers, so the three of us shared them in rotation. When Mother died, one of the covers became of great sentimental value to me. I kept it close to me following her death, and for many years, it gave me some much-needed comfort during some very dark days. I still have this cover, one of the few things I have from my childhood. I occasionally come across it in the cupboard and find myself smiling, knowing that my mother is still watching over me and helping me on my journey. When I think of the hard life she endured, I realize how fortunate I am now to have a comfortable lifestyle, with a caring family and a career that I love. Every day, I vow to capture every opportunity that comes my way and, more importantly, to do my best to make sure that Risa, now a teenager, does the same.

Chapter 5

To Wed or Not to Wed

I was now aged seventeen and in my second year of college. It was summer holiday, and I was working at the municipal swimming pool, selling entry tickets. Many other students took up summer jobs there, some of whom were training to be physical education teachers and worked as lifeguards, all competing for attention as they modeled themselves on the handsome lifeguards patrolling beaches in popular television programs. It was there that I met a boy four years my senior named An Cheng, known as Chen, and we started dating. He

1987. Pei and boyfriend Chen.

was studying at the National Normal University in the Faculty of Physical Education and was training to be a teacher. He was from a hardworking, humble family in the countryside, his hometown being a four-hour journey south of Taiwan. His father made tofu to sell at local markets. (Tofu is a popular food made from mashed soya beans and commonly used in vegetarian cooking.) Chen was just what I needed at that stage in my life: he was gentle, loving, and kind, and he made me feel special, something I had never really known. I felt safe with him.

We slipped into an easy, safe relationship, with no quarrels or demands, and dated for three years. We got on well together and planned to get married one day. In addition to being at college all day, I worked on weekends and in the evenings as a waitress; still, he would patiently wait for me to finish my shifts, never complaining. During my last year of college, I often dreamed of the day we would get married and live together in the countryside. I even chose names for our children. For me, Chen represented stability: it was almost as if he had been sent to fill the void left by my mother.

When Chen graduated from university, he was drafted into the military for two years of compulsory national service, followed by one year of compulsory teaching, as required by the government. I graduated from college in 1987, when I was twenty years old, and found work with an Australian import/export company.

Life in Taiwan was changing: martial law was now officially over after the longest run in world history. There was an atmosphere of optimism among young people. On the other hand, older people were understandably more cautious, the oppression of the last almost forty years being fresh in their minds. And for elderly people who had also lived under Japanese rule, it was difficult to believe that their lives would ever change for the better. What we didn't know then was that in about twenty years, Taiwan would emerge as an

1990. Pei, row two, second from the right, at the Buddhist College studying to become a monk.

economic powerhouse, evolving away from the grip of dictatorship and into a democracy, offering opportunity and freedom to younger generations, especially to women.

It was about four years since my mother's death and by now, although I still missed her, I had come to terms with her no longer being a physical presence in my life. The same went for my other deceased family members. I was much different from the depressed teenager I once was, not least of all thanks to Chen, who had helped tremendously to pull me through the loneliness and despair. He promised to always look after me. But although happier than in past years, I was still spiritually lost and was trying hard to find a purpose in life.

As I began working for the Australian import/export company during the daytime, I decided to enroll in a course at night school, along with my first sister and my school friend Sarah, to study Buddhism. The course was taught by two female monks. Upon learning of my interest in Buddhism, a colleague suggested I should

1990. Pei, second from the left, preparing for commitment to life as a monk.

meet Victor Wu, who used to work for the Australian company before I joined. He had recently resigned from his job to study Buddhism and was now training to be a monk.

I got in touch with Victor Wu, and all of us (Victor, my first sister, Sarah, and me) attended evening classes in Buddhism for the next five years. During that period, Victor completed his studies and started living as a monk, calling himself *Shih* Wu Hung. It was also during this time that the four of us and our two teachers started to research issues relating to human rights, the treatment of prisoners, and domestic violence. We put together information packs and actively campaigned for individuals afflicted by clear instances of injustice. Of the cases we worked on, one centered around a migrant worker from China who was sentenced to death for killing his Taiwanese boss in self-defense. With the Taiwanese police and courts' pervasive prejudice against China working against the offender, it was nigh impossible for him to have a fair trial. Another case concerned women who had had abortions and were persuaded to give money to a religious cult to ensure their aborted babies' reincarnation, believing that they would otherwise be doomed to a lifetime of bad luck. This was not an unusual situation: pregnant women were often blackmailed into giving large sums of money to unscrupulous criminals in the name of religion.

In addition, I completed an evening course in counseling for young offenders, and for two years, I was a volunteer counselor for Taipei City Council. I could relate to some of these young people: many of their problems reminded me of my own during my teenage years. I didn't realize it at the time, but experiences like this would become the foundation for my future career campaigning against injustice affecting humans, other animal species, and the environment. I also spent two years studying Christianity, which teaches that we have one life and one chance to do things right, in contrast to the endless cycle of birth and rebirth and reincarnation in Buddhism. Even though I did not believe in God or want to become a Christian, I was intrigued by different belief systems; my curiosity about Christianity also unexpectedly led me to a different arena when I joined the Christian church's flower-arranging course, which was fulfilling in its own way. I found that I greatly appreciated the beauty and intrigue of the varied shapes and shades of plants and flowers, and that I had a flair for arranging them in beautiful displays. Within a year, I had found a business partner, and together, we opened a florist shop in Taipei. My work with the Australian company also opened new horizons in my mind as I began to learn about life in other countries. I became fascinated with traditions and cultures elsewhere in the world, so different from the ones I had grown up with.

In 1992, my former evening-class teachers, the two female monks with whom I did volunteer work, founded an organization called the Life Conservationist Association (LCA), and I became the first

LCA staff member. My employment was financially supported by Mr. Chang, a Buddhist benefactor who owned the building where the LCA had its office, who generously let us use his space and equipment and has since become a lifelong friend. Eventually, Wu Hung was sent by his master to work at the LCA, while my first sister and my friend Sarah became volunteers.

It was the LCA's mission to stand up against all injustice, with the belief that all living things are equal. Before we took any action on the streets or in the media, we researched and analyzed information extensively; our independent findings often sharply contrasted the emotional rhetoric advanced by media outlets. One of our early campaigns involved signature-collecting actions and street demonstrations to oppose the government's ongoing plans to construct a fourth nuclear power station on the island. The LCA joined with more than one thousand Buddhists to hold an all-night

1992. Pei, 1st row, 3rd from right, with LCA supporters outside the Legislative Yuan in Taipei, staging an all-night silent protest against the construction of a 4th nuclear power station.

1992. Pei collecting signatures in protest against the Chinese bear bile products on sale in Taiwan.

silent vigil outside the Legislative Yuan (the Parliament) building in Taipei. Another campaign protested against the poor living conditions of the animals at Taipei Zoo. Yet another condemned the keeping of fish in an overcrowded, artificial indoor pool. For entertainment, people could pay to throw a metal hook into the pool to catch a fish; often, the fish had hooks become embedded into their body parts and the wounds become infected. The owners of the pool, wanting the fish to stay alive so they could be caught another day, put antibiotics into the water—a situation made worse by the fact that there was no legislation at the time to control such medications.

Influenced by this type of work, I had grown into a young woman with a new perspective on life by the time Chen finished his compulsory national service. He, on the other hand, although happy for me as I had found some fulfillment in life and interested to hear all about my experiences, was keen to get married and settle down in the peaceful countryside.

Naturally, I was not ready to give up city life and the social justice campaigns I had been working on for the past few years, and I was hungry for more knowledge about the world. I loved Chen as a dear friend, but I felt his pond was too small for me. Had I outgrown him? We continued to date. He began to study for a master's degree at Taipei University, while I became more involved with Buddhist activities and found that working on human rights issues and helping others gave me a sense of worth and achievement. But with my full-time work occupying my days, volunteer work taking up evenings and weekends, plus work on my business (the florist shop), I was an often elusive and unreliable girlfriend.

One day, Chen said: "I need you to make a decision. We have been together for six years and I want to marry you, but you don't seem as if you want to commit, and I feel I can't wait any longer. I am asking you to decide." I fully understood his frustration: being the only son in his family, he felt it was his duty to get married and have children to carry on the family name. So I heard myself saying, "Yes, I do want to get married." Why did I say that when I was thinking the opposite?

Ecstatic, he took the bus back home to tell his parents. On the way home, he rang me to ask if I was sure, and I replied that I was. Again, why did I say yes—why couldn't I be honest with him? I will never understand. I knew that I did not want to marry anyone at that stage. I did love Chen, but not enough to marry him then. When he got to his parents' home and told his family of our plans to wed, an uncle said to him: "Don't marry her. She has kept you dangling for six years; she is not the right one for you." More than anything, I was relieved to hear that his uncle had put doubts in Chen's mind. We decided not to rush into marriage and continued dating on and off for the next few years.

As much as I loved volunteering with the LCA, which helped put my ingrained self-pity at the back of my mind, I was working long hours on investigations and publicity campaigns. Yet Chen would sit around for all those hours, not a word of complaint coming out of him, waiting for me to go through the never-ending pile of work on my desk.

One day, Chen told me he had started seeing someone else and was returning to the countryside. He'd become friendly with a volunteer he'd met while waiting for me at the LCA office. Having waited patiently for me for, altogether, almost ten years, he knew at this point that our marriage was not going to happen. Our breakup was swift. Somewhat relieved at the time, I focused on my work and dedicated even more of my time to the LCA's mission. Then, about a year later, a dream about Chen made me realize what a wonderful man I had lost. Over the next few weeks, as I thought of him more and more, I began to miss him dearly. Finally, one day, I called and asked to see him. He told me he had gotten married the day before.

Devastated, I cried nonstop. It felt just like another bereavement; the pain was excruciating. I felt so guilty for having been so thoughtless and unkind to him when he had never failed to show me love and commitment. Looking back, I can see that because I'd had no role model to prepare me for lifelong commitment to another person, the thought of it frightened me. I began cutting myself—repeatedly, on my arms—as a way of inflicting pain as punishment for my selfish and thoughtless behavior. I felt so alone: I didn't have parents, nor could I talk to my sisters or my brother as their situations were so different from mine. We had drifted even further apart during the past ten years, and they were all either married or in long-term relationships.

Once again, my life was floundering. I convinced myself that I was a bad person and that I did not deserve good things in life. Once again, suicide was hovering in the front of my mind. I was scared and needed to belong to someone or something. I decided to live at a Buddhist temple and devote my life to doing public service as a monk. It was here that I found the peace and isolation to think rationally and unravel the complexities of my earlier years.

Eventually, it was time for me to be measured for my robe—one of the final steps before I was to have my head shaved and live as a monk. I was excited; I thought I was ready. But was I really? Suddenly, doubts began to creep into my mind. After much soul-searching, I decided I wasn't. Thankfully, no one tried to persuade me one way or the other. My decision was respected, and I continued to work at the LCA. I realize now that although I was desperately searching for a purpose in life, monkhood was not the right pathway for me. Nonetheless, the years of Buddhist studies have proven to be an ideal training ground for my current work with ACTAsia, for which I am often working alone for long periods, focusing on priority tasks.

But let's get back to the story of my relationship with Chen. Fast forward almost thirty years to 2019, I was visiting Taiwan, and as I was staying in Taipei for a few days, ACTAsia staff had arranged for me to give a presentation on sustainable fashion at a museum close to the area where Chen lived. Over the years, whenever he came to mind, I always found myself becoming uncomfortable and feeling intense embarrassment. It was one of my big regrets in life—not that I didn't marry him but that I had not been honest with him about my thoughts and feelings—and I will always feel ashamed of my behavior toward him.

After much deliberation, I decided that as I was in the area, I would message Chen and ask if we could meet. If he didn't reply or declined my invitation, it was understandable. So I took the plunge. Much to my delight and relief, he came to my hotel at 7 p.m. that evening, and we were able to speak freely, with no awkwardness. The years seemed to just roll away. It was in some ways like old times and in other ways different; we were no longer in our twenties but in our fifties, hopefully both older and wiser. Chen and his wife were successful in their careers at the university, and he was now an assistant professor. I told him how sorry I was for the way I had treated him all those years ago. He smiled as he said: "If you had married me, you wouldn't have built an international organization and be here today to give this presentation. I'm also sorry as I broke my promise to you. I promised I would look after you for all of your life, but then chose someone else instead."

The next morning, as I was preparing to leave the hotel, he arrived with a gift of some local delicacies for me to share with my sisters in Taipei. His time was limited as he was teaching that morning, so our conversation was brief, but he was still the same kind, caring person I remembered with such fondness from all those years ago. It was me who had changed. I know that I did once love him, but that I was too confused and self-centered at the time to know what I wanted, instead taking advantage of his kind nature. I had a lot to learn about humanity and selfless love.

I have no regrets about the outcome of our relationship—it was not meant to last forever—but I still feel disappointed with myself for the way I treated Chen without any thought for his needs. He has so graciously forgiven me, but I'm not sure I have forgiven myself.

My first love story was a poignant one. For ten years, a long time in the lives of young people, Chen was there for me when I needed him most. I still feel a close connection to him in a spiritual sense, and I am so thankful we had an opportunity to heal past hurt. Our contact now consists of birthday wishes exchanged on social media.

Chapter 6

Buddhism and the Life Conservationist Association

Having decided against becoming a monk, I once again threw myself into the work of the LCA, believing this was the best use of my time and energy. Buddhism and its belief that all life is equal were at the center of everything we did and discussed. At the time, I was not particularly preoccupied with animal issues or even really understood why animal welfare was a specific concern, but it did make sense to me to have a mission based on justice for all forms of life.

During a visit to Taipei Zoo, I could see that some animals appeared to be bored and unsettled from the way they paced up and down in their enclosures. I could see that the polar bear was suffering from some type of severe skin infection, with scabs and pustular eruptions covering his head and parts of his body. Even so, I was not aware that the hot and humid climate in Taiwan, coupled with the confines of a concrete enclosure, was unsuitable for a polar bear. I now cringe at my past ignorance, but as I gradually began to consider the depth and richness of the lives of animals, that marked the start of a new chapter in my life. I began to question the existence of zoos, often asking my colleagues, "Why is it that an animal who naturally roams the land and waters of such a cold area as the Arctic region is transported across the world to live as an exhibit in totally unsuitable conditions?"

1995. Polar bear in Taipei Zoo with skin infection.
Credit: Life Conservationist Association, Taiwan.

A visit to Taiwan in 1993 by the Environmental Investigation Agency (EIA), an experienced and knowledgeable organization, gave the LCA a great boost. The EIA team—Peter Knight, Steve Galster, and David Bowles from the UK, joined by Alan Carr from the partner organization in the US—had come to Taiwan to investigate the illegal trades in rhino horn, ivory, and orangutans. The LCA was approached and asked to share our local knowledge. We were eager to help in any way we could. In return, we were amazed to learn of the extent of the international wildlife trade, with live animals and animal parts being smuggled through many countries and across many borders. We learned that the trade in rhino horn was unregulated, with a known route from Africa to Taiwan, where there was a demand for rhino horn to be ground into a powder and used in the production of traditional

Chinese medicine (TCM). Globally, Taiwan was the largest market for rhino horn, which many people believed could cure common illnesses such as meningitis, arthritis, headaches, gout, boils, and even anxiety. Rhino horn is a keratin structure much like human hair and fingernails—simply put, nothing more than compacted hair—yet it is so prized in Taiwan that its value equals that of gold.

Inspired by the EIA's visit, the LCA started to focus on the illegal wildlife trade, which to date still represents the greatest threat to the world's vulnerable biodiversity. We recognized how widespread cultural superstitions could have negative global repercussions and work against science-based species conservation efforts. In 1993, the demand in Asia for rhino-horn powder was causing the massacre of rhinos in Africa, with massive numbers of rhino carcasses being left to rot after the removal of just the horns. People believed that this powder was more effective than antibiotics at reducing fever-induced meningitis. At present, with many still believing that rhino horn can cure cancer, families would buy a rhino horn together and grind it into powder, then share it among themselves for safekeeping, to be used when needed. Although Taiwan imposed a ban on trading rhino horn in 1993, this supposed cure-all continued to be readily available on the black market. Despite the fact that numerous studies and experiments carried out over many years have found no curative or medicinal benefits, much of Asia still chooses to ignore the science and buy into the myth of the magical rhino horn.

Likewise, the trade in ivory was banned in 1990, but it continued to be smuggled into China via Taiwan. Ivory—a hard, white substance made up of mainly dentine and produced from the teeth and tusks of mammals such as elephants and walruses—is used for ornamental purposes in the mass production of jewelry and souvenirs, as well as for piano keys. In 1986, a television program known as *The Naughty Family* became very popular in Taiwan. This hugely successful show, featuring an orangutan called Hsiao Li, portrayed the animal as the ideal family companion. As a result, keeping orangutans as pets became fashionable, and demand in Taiwan skyrocketed. According to a report from *New Scientist* in 1984, an estimated 1,000 young orangutans were illegally imported into Taiwan and sold as pets, mainly through newspaper advertisements. Other wild animal species that also became fashionable as pets included crocodiles, cobras, muntjac, tigers, and bears. It was not unusual to see either a bear or a tiger kept in a cage outside a shop to attract customers.

It was not until a few years later that there was any concrete action to stop the trade in orangutans in Taiwan, but in 1989, an important step was taken when the Wildlife Conservation Law was passed, requiring owners to register their animals. Around 3,000 orangutans were registered, but many owners ignored the new law, and the real number of these animals in captivity was thought to be closer to 1,000. Some of the animals were found to be infected with

1992. A baby bear kept as a pet in Taiwan.

2001. Bear gall bladder, claws, and teeth, as used in TCM.

hepatitis B and tuberculosis, almost certainly caught from humans. Many were abandoned by their owners, either from fear of disease or because of the orangutans' unpredictable and aggressive behavior as they reached sexual maturity.

Following the EIA investigations, Victor Watkins, a zoologist and Director of Wildlife at the World Society for the Protection of Animals (WSPA) in London, came to Taiwan to research the trade in bear bile for use mainly in TCM. Like the EIA, he asked for some of the LCA's local knowledge, which we were only too keen to give as it was an ideal opportunity to establish international connections. We were hungry for all the precious information and knowledge we could gain from having such connections, as Taiwan was still a young country with limited international exposure. Thanks to the visits by the EIA and WSPA, Wu Hung and I, together with our colleagues at the LCA, learned of the corruption and the network of countless trading routes passing through many countries that contributed to the illegal trade in wild animals and wild-animal products used in the production of TCM.

We discussed other animal-related issues, including the stray dog problem throughout Taiwan, with Victor, who explained that many countries had a similar problem. In fact, the World Health Organization (WHO) and WSPA had conducted a global survey and produced a report with recommendations to governments for the humane management of stray and unwanted dogs. He promised to send us a copy. Historically, government authorities tended to take no action with regard to stray dogs unless there was an outbreak of rabies, livestock were attacked or killed, or humans were attacked or killed. When one of those events occurred, local governments would send teams of dog catchers to shoot or poison the dogs, or else remove them using brutal, inhumane methods. This type of response caused friction within communities, provoked international condemnation, and incurred significant costs for governments from having to fund "killing squads" and specialized equipment.

With so many issues of concern in Taiwan, what could the LCA do to help? We needed to widen our knowledge base and understanding of animal welfare and learn why humans continued to abuse animals. What were the reasons? Was it because of ignorance, greed, indifference, tradition, or deliberate cruelty? Or, perhaps, a complex combination of several of these factors? We had a lot to learn.

Following the EIA and WSPA's visits, the LCA decided to research and investigate what wild-animal products were being sold on the market. We needed to determine the demand for such products and the size of the wildlife trade in Taiwan. I was excited to be part of the team. Through desk research, I learned that many Asians believed that consuming wild-animal parts, such as tiger bone, rhino horn, bear gallbladder, bear bile, snake blood, snake meat, sea turtle meat, and turtle shell, would magically heal their illnesses and enhance their strength.

In Taipei, we had an area known as Snake Alley at the night market in Wanhua District; I knew that wild-animal parts were sold at the many restaurants serving traditional Taiwanese dishes there. Live snakes were killed and skinned on the spot and cooked in front of patrons, to be served with snake blood cocktails, turtle blood, and deer penis wine. I had never questioned where the animals came from, probably thinking they weren't any different from other animals eaten by humans. I had never visited Snake Alley: my mother always told me and my sisters to keep away from the area as it was also a red-light district, with pornography shops, striptease artists performing in dimly lit booths that lined the streets, and scantily clothed prostitutes parading outside the brothels to entice punters.

Although we had no training in investigative work, several of us from the LCA set off with lots of enthusiasm and more than a smattering of ignorance. We had no equipment other than a camera. We went to the Wanhua night market, then we went from town to town, surveying other markets where wild animals and wild-animal parts could be purchased. In addition, as dog eating was still popular at the time, there were markets where dogs were cramped in cages, waiting to be slaughtered as buyers wanted fresh meat. Such markets were always busy. There was no effective animal protection law in Taiwan at the time, so any species of animals could be made available for consumption if there was demand. And we could reasonably assume that this demand came from mainly locals, as it was unusual to see any Western faces in Taiwan in the early 1990s, trade and tourism still being in their infancy.

Back at the LCA office, we collated the information and prepared to hold street protests. We used posters and banners to attract attention and put pressure on the authorities to take action. This type of demonstrations was quite new in Taiwan, so ours attracted attention from the media.

Sometimes, we also rescued animals such as dogs or monkeys from the markets, but the problem then was finding someone willing to keep them. Sometimes, the police were called and told us to stop; some of us were, on occasion, arrested. Often, members of the public shouted at us and ridiculed our actions. In retrospect, we were either incredibly brave or incredibly stupid: we could have so easily gotten jail time for "disturbing the peace" or been considered anti-establishment. Fortunately, as the LCA was run by Buddhist monks, the authorities concerned were not sure how to deal with us, so if anyone was arrested, they were usually released before having to appear in court.

I was beginning to learn how cultural beliefs could significantly compromise attempts to create change. I eventually came to the realization that although protests and rescues could be effective in the short term and relieve immediate suffering, sustainable change required education—we must change the hearts and minds of people, so that the cycle of abuse afflicting humans, animals, and the environment would eventually cease. Our way of doing investigative work was amateur and naïve, but at the time, we thought it was revolutionary. In discussions among our team at the LCA, we raised the question, "Why doesn't Taiwan have any effective legislation to control people's behavior toward animals?" Under martial law, Taiwanese people had had their behavior and activities tightly controlled and faced severe punishments if they had failed to comply. Surely, it could not be that difficult to instill humane treatment of animals into civic society, right?

But it was 1993: we had been free of martial law for just four years, and new laws for a new Taiwan had yet to be drafted and implemented. We needed to find out how the population's attitudes could be changed and how legislation could hold animal abusers responsible.

1999. Wu Hung with a friendly cat.

Through discussions with EIA and WSPA personnel, we learned that the US and countries in Europe had comprehensive animal protection laws; we realized it was essential for us to find out how these came into being. As it turned out, regardless of the country, a two-pronged approach is always needed, the two prongs being legislation to hold people responsible and public education to enable people to understand why it is important to follow the law. With so many factors to consider, Wu Hung and I decided to visit prominent organizations in the US on a fact-finding mission. But how could we arrange this?

At the time, there were no directories in Taiwan of organizations working on animal welfare or humane education. Moreover, my spoken English was poor, as I had never had the opportunity to communicate with English speakers; Wu Hung's English was only slightly better. Luckily, thanks to our previous business training at the Australian trading company, we knew how to conduct research and quickly built a list of potential organizations to visit. We approached our upcoming travels as one would a business project as we had only a small, fixed budget and limited time to cover thousands of miles and several countries. We needed a plan of action. Without realizing it at the time, we were about to embark on a journey to a different world. An eye-opener was in store for us!

It was a short while after the LCA was established, and we were trying to decide what our focus of work should be for the coming years. Other individuals and small groups in Taiwan were starting to think about the plight of animals, many of them wanting to save dogs from the streets or learn how to protect animals in the wild. No one, however, seemed to have any interest in the care and welfare of farmed animals. So we decided that the LCA would focus on farmed animal welfare and that when visiting organizations in the US, we would gather information from people already working on factory farming issues.

In 1994, we left our homeland, where one could count on one hand the number of NGOs working for the protection of humans and animals, for countries where animal welfare standards were upheld by the law, with many organizations working to strengthen and improve the very same legislation. A new world opened up to us, a world where so many people not only believed in treating all animals, irrespective of species, with respect and kindness, but also worked to promote guidelines and policies for the management of animals in various settings, including zoos, circuses, farms, laboratories, slaughterhouses, domestic residences, and the wild.

Once in the US, we visited the Animal Welfare Institute (AWI), Farm Sanctuary, the Humane Society of the United States of

America (HSUS), the Massachusetts Society for the Prevention of Cruelty to Animals (MSPCA), the American Society for Prevention of Cruelty to Animals (ASPCA), People for the Ethical Treatment of Animals (PETA), and the International Society of Animal Rights. We also attended meetings on the Convention for International Trade in Endangered Species (CITES) at the United Nations building in New York.

We returned to Taiwan with our heads overflowing with new knowledge and understandings, along with numerous books, brochures, and films to help us plan the next stage of the LCA's actions in Taiwan. But most importantly, although still amateurs, we now had a steely determination to transform animal welfare in our country, inspired by so many people at the professional organizations we had visited, who had generously given their time to talk with us and to whom I will always be grateful.

Having been exposed to an entirely different way of thinking, we were now gradually beginning to process our new experiences. We now understood that animals have intrinsic value, that they are sentient beings with senses and emotions just as are humans. We now understood that it is humankind's responsibility to show respect and consideration for all forms of life, as people, animals, and the environment are interrelated and interdependent. This new way of thinking made complete sense.

We were steeped in Buddhist philosophy, whose mantra "all life is equal" is easy to say but not so easy to translate into real life. However, with the understanding that legislation and education provide the basis for changing people's attitudes and behaviors, we had now added a practical component to our philosophy, and the idea of the interconnected world was beginning to really resonate. Our travels had enlightened us and cemented our early roles as part of a global movement.

Inspired and eager to act anew, the LCA decided to immediately conduct a large-scale field study of farmed animals in Taiwan, joining forces with a film college to document the factory farming industry. We had little idea at the time of the misery and suffering we would uncover. Our findings showing pigs, cows, and chickens housed in cramped, poorly ventilated facilities and slaughtered through inhumane methods proved beyond doubt the industry's cruelty and lack of concern for these animals' welfare. At the same time, the film *Crying Life*, released in 1994, became of great interest to those in the Buddhist community (wherein many people were already vegetarian or vegan), internationally and especially in Taiwan. The film was regularly shown at temples, and for the first time in Taiwan, people started to think about their eating habits and how their food was produced, with many choosing to convert to vegetarianism. In retrospect, Wu Hung and I could be considered pioneers, plunging into this work at a time when most people in Asia had no understanding of terms such as "animal welfare," "animal sentience," or "humane treatment."

In less than ten years, the LCA was the leading animal welfare organization in Taiwan and spearheading the drive for an updated animal protection law, which was eventually passed in 2018. Our work helped bring about the regulation of animal markets such as those in Snake Alley, as well as the closing of the last snake-meat restaurant. Some of LCA staff eventually branched out and formed an organization known as Environment and Animal Society of Taiwan (EAST), led by Wu Hung, which now collaborates with local and international NGOs on global issues. EAST is well respected for its thorough work on a wide range of issues, in particular its investigations and projects on intensive animal farming, which poses the largest animal welfare problem of all and is also a main contributor to climate change, with implications for the future of our planet that are of utmost concern.

1995. LCA/WSPA Pet Respect Conference with government officials; Disposable Dogs: Made in Taiwan.

On a personal note, along with Buddhism, Wu Hung had a major hand in my growth. Dressed in his monk's robe, he certainly caught the attention of people during his visits to Western countries, as it was rare to see a monk doing what he did. Relentless yet patient and considerate, he was able to handle any situation, be it challenging the government on social justice issues, being questioned by the media, speaking at conferences, or training his team of volunteers. He was charismatic, sincere, and a good listener—an approachable leader and an amiable companion. His logical thinking and backbone of steel in spite of his quiet, unassuming manner helped influence and shape my own behavior and reasoning. I was fortunate to have Wu Hung as my mentor and friend for many years. Even now, thirty years later, I still often look to what he taught me for guidance.

Chapter 7

International Connections

The year 1994 marked one of the LCA's most significant milestones—a project that rocked the world of dog lovers and, moreover, the Taiwanese government. Known as "Disposable Dogs: Made in Taiwan," the project began as an initiative between the LCA and WSPA.

Taiwan, an emerging economic powerhouse, was now forging ahead with its industrial plan in a period of rapid economic growth and industrialization known as the Taiwan Miracle. With an economy largely based on science and technology, Taiwan became one of the Four Asian Tigers, the others being Hong Kong, South Korea, and Singapore.

But despite this explosive industrial development, social development in Taiwan seemed to be overlooked. Foreigners coming to Taiwan in search of investment opportunities or simply as tourists often commented on the overcrowded roads, the erratic driving, and also the numerous stray dogs roaming the busy streets and causing chaos. Even Tripadvisor, the well-known international tourist guide, warned of stray dogs on the main roads in Taipei causing accidents, attacking each other in competition for food from the countless street vendor's stalls, and sometimes even attacking people.

When the municipality received complaints from the public, dog catchers were sent onto the streets to capture the dogs, using thin-wire nooses that cut deep into the necks of the animals. This was done in full view of the public. Captured dogs were then thrown into a vehicle and taken to the local municipal garbage dump, where they were kept in either a cage or a pit and left to starve to death. To most of us today, this sounds extremely cruel. However, this was almost thirty years ago in Taiwan: these animals were regarded not as living beings but as rubbish—disposable and unwanted—so it seemed logical for them to be treated as such. Not only was humane euthanasia for these unwanted animals not an option then, but ironically, it was believed that a person who would perform it would suffer in the afterlife. Leaving an animal to suffer and die a slow, agonizing death, on the other hand, was not in the least condemnable.

Working for the LCA, Wu Hung and I decided to find out exactly where in Taiwan the unwanted dogs were taken. Did the government have a policy for the management of the stray dog population, or was it decided at the local level? One day, we followed the dog-catching vehicle and watched as the dog catchers skillfully cornered and pounced on dogs roaming main streets, using the wire nooses to prevent them from escaping. Howls of distress filled the air as the wires sank into the dogs' necks, sometimes slicing ears or muzzles if caught in the fur of heavier-coated dogs.

It was upsetting to watch, and we had to try our hardest to restrain ourselves from shouting at the workers and demanding that they leave the dogs alone. We needed to learn all we could about how these animals were dealt with. Some dogs put up a good fight, snapping and snarling threateningly at their captors. But others just seemed resigned to their fate and offered little resistance.

Once the vehicle was fully loaded with an assortment of dogs—any who could be caught, as type and size were of no importance—it then traveled to a garbage dump outside the city. Keeping a safe distance behind—but careful not to lose sight of—the municipal vehicle, we watched through binoculars, all the while still hearing the dogs' squeals of pain and terror, as they were unloaded and thrown into cages. Once their mission was complete, the men drove away in their empty vehicle.

When we were sure the dog catchers were well away from the site, we hurriedly approached the area where we could see several rusty and dilapidated wire cages. What a horrific sight met our eyes! In many of the cages were dead dogs, some half eaten by other dogs in the same cage. Some were still alive—just barely—but were past the point of no return. Many had weeping sores where the nooses were still embedded into their necks. A heavily pregnant dog—some type of spaniel—looked up at us with woeful eyes.

Other than taking photographs and documenting all that we saw, we were unable to do anything to help the animals. We had no resources or facilities, nor did we know of any animal shelters. We did not know how to handle these dogs; perhaps some of them were aggressive or had transmissible diseases. We had been raised and were living in a culture that put street dogs in the same category as rats and other "vermin," so no veterinary service was likely to offer any assistance, such services being reserved for farmed animals at the time. Just a few veterinarians in Taipei and other large cities such as Kaohsiung were beginning to see purebred dogs due to increasing demand from wealthy owners, but street dogs were not seen as members of even the same species.

With no better option we could think of, we resorted to our usual MO, exposing the situation in the media with incriminating photos and marching through the city in protest. But few people paid attention; after all, in the eyes of the public, the dogs were "vermin" and needed to be exterminated. We were deemed crazy, irrational people who were making a fuss over nothing. In a statement, a municipal spokesperson suggested the photos were fakes but said he would investigate the matter and make sure there was no mismanagement or any other wrongdoing.

1995. Typical government facilities for stray dogs, mass overcrowding.

The LCA decided the stray-dog situation should be thoroughly looked into and asked the EIA if they would take on such an investigation, but as the latter was focusing on wildlife issues, they suggested we should contact the headquarters of the WSPA in London. We took their advice, and in response, the WSPA sent Joy Leney to Taipei to meet with us and assess the problem. Joy was the WSPA's International Projects Director and had just set up a new campaign known as Pet Respect. As she explained to us, before starting any project, it's necessary to establish the size and scale of the problem at hand, whether it is localized or spread over a wider area, and if there is any ongoing response by the government, organizations, or individuals. In our case, there was no one simple method of managing the problem as we needed a combination of legislation, registration and identification of owned dogs, spay/neuter services, and education. But nothing could be implemented and enforced unless there was collaboration and cooperation with officials from the central government, municipalities, public health authorities, veterinarians, schools, public educators, and the media. Our problem was a complex mix, so there would be no quick fix.

We arranged meetings between Joy and government officials, who, although we were able to show photographic evidence to the contrary, assured us that they considered the issue to be important and would make sure that their policies were humane, that no mistreatment of the animals would happen again. We had introduced the Five Freedoms to the government when working on animal farming issues; we were now showing officials how a similar principle could be applied to the management of dogs and all other species in captivity. The Five Freedoms—the first widely accepted animal welfare framework—first came about after a 1965 British parliamentary inquiry into the treatment of animals on intensive farms, focusing on the key physical needs of each animal. Importantly, the Freedoms were later updated and rewritten to include psychological needs and are still in use today.

1996. A government facility for stray dogs, a hole in the ground on a garbage site.

Experience told us that despite these empty promises from government officials, we needed to investigate all of the various collection sites in Taiwan and gather photographic evidence that could not be disputed. It was agreed that Joy would return to Taiwan in a few months to carry out a countrywide survey and investigation with LCA personnel and an international vet. Meanwhile, Asir, one of the LCA's volunteers, would travel around Taiwan to identify sites where dogs were taken after being collected from the streets.

Once Asir had completed his preliminary survey, Joy returned to Taiwan and the investigation began. During a four-week period, we traveled to all municipalities in Taiwan, surveying more than seventy-five sites where there were holding facilities for captured stray dogs (we combined some of the smaller areas with neighboring districts for our survey). These facilities were mainly holes in the ground at garbage dumps, broken and rusty wire cages, and overcrowded pens in government yards. Again, some of the animals we found were already dead and some were being eaten. The dogs weren't provided with food or water, so they were gradually starving to death. Although this was the fate for many of the dogs, at other sites, we discovered dogs being disposed of by various inhumane methods of euthanasia, including by the use of gas chambers, electric chambers, and drowning. Euthanasia by drowning was achieved by overcrowded cages containing dogs being hoisted and plunged into large tanks of water.

Following collection and collation, our findings were taken to the appropriate government department. At first, the Taiwanese government was in denial, again accusing us of faking the photos and footage. The LCA decided to release the findings to the Taiwanese media, as well as in other countries through our international contacts. Thanks to international pressure supporting pressure coming from within the country, the Taiwanese government gradually came

1992. An orangutan kept as a pet in Taipei.

to accept our findings and agree that such inhumane treatment of living beings should stop. This time holding the government accountable for its promise, the LCA kept exposing and checking on municipalities relentlessly until all of them were officially instructed to stop destroying stray dogs in the old ways, instead to build facilities where the animals would be housed and treated humanely.

The Taiwanese government cooperated with the LCA and international experts on numerous animal welfare initiatives, funding training courses and workshops for animal handlers, shelter managers, and animal welfare inspectors, as well as introducing humane education into schools. Government personnel also worked alongside experts from national NGOs to prepare the new animal protection law, the most comprehensive and progressive legislation in the Asian region. Yet another significant milestone was the introduction of the drug pentobarbitone, recommended internationally as a humane method of euthanasia for dogs. Humane methods of slaughter for animals farmed for human consumption were also introduced.

The LCA-WSPA Pet Respect campaign "Disposable Dogs: Made in Taiwan" was a turning point in the history of animal welfare advocacy in Taiwan, with the terms "animal welfare" and "animal sentience" starting to acquire meaning among the public. But even today, Taiwanese culture and society still need to engender more compassion and respect for people, animals, and the environment. There is still a long way to go.

* * *

One day, while traveling with Joy to a government meeting, I nervously asked if she thought I would be able to study abroad, fully expecting her to advise me to think again, carefully and cautiously. To my surprise, she immediately exclaimed, "Of course!" I explained to her that I thought I could gain so much knowledge about animal welfare and humane education from Western countries to then introduce to Taiwan. Joy was incredibly encouraging and supportive; she didn't try to dampen my thoughts by telling me that my English skills were poor or that I would need lots of money. She gave me the confidence boost that I needed to first think, then say out loud, "Perhaps my dream of studying abroad is not so unreachable!"

On my twenty-seventh birthday, I secretly made a promise to myself. I vowed that by my thirtieth birthday, I would be living and working abroad. How this would happen I had little idea at the time, but I was determined to make my wish come true.

By the beginning of 1995, I was in regular contact with people in many different countries. Some of these connections came from my research; others came from those who were following animal welfare developments in Taiwan and offering help. I knew by now that this work to bring about justice for people, animals, and the environment was my calling. I wanted to travel, learn all I could about the world, and work in other countries. I wanted to find out if I had the ability and determination to work for a cause without the tenacity and support of Wu Hung to guide me. But I felt I still lacked confidence. I was just a young woman with no academic title. I didn't have a zoology or biology degree or any veterinary qualifications. How could I get a job that would let me be taken seriously by government authorities and the media? More and more questions abounded: Would my experience in Taiwan be relevant in a Western context? If I left Taiwan, would I be able to adapt to another culture? Where would I even go?

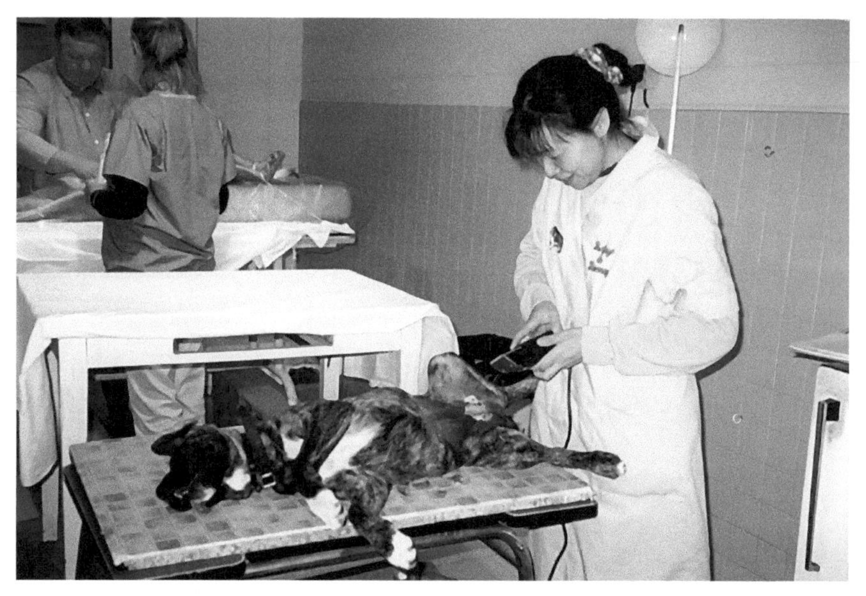

1997. Pei learning to prepare an animal for an operation at Refuge de Thiernay training course.

Chapter 8

Destiny Calling

One day in 1995, a friend and I decided to go to the cinema to see a new film that was being promoted. It was called *Braveheart* and billed as a historical drama loosely based on the life of William Wallace, a Scottish knight who led the Scots into battle with King Edward I of England in the late thirteenth century.

At the time, my friend was studying ornithology—in particular the red kite, a bird of prey from the same family as eagles and buzzards. The promotion of the film, which showed scenes of the wild, rugged landscape of Scotland, appealed to him as the red kite was about to be reintroduced into Scotland, having been hunted to extinction there in the nineteenth century. As for me, I was also intrigued by how Scotland was portrayed in the trailers and on billboards, with seemingly endless miles of open countryside, in such sharp contrast to the crowded island of Taiwan.

Watching the film, I was suddenly overcome with a strong feeling of déjà vu. Scotland seemed so familiar to me, and I immediately felt as if I had been to this country in a former life. I have always believed in reincarnation; in that moment, the film all but vindicated my belief. I sensed that I had lived in Scotland and been married to a Scot. The landscape, the clothing, the music, and even the accent were all so familiar to me, which was so strange given I could barely understand the English language!

1996. Princess Elisabeth de Croÿ with Panchaio, a dog she rescued from Taiwan when visiting as an animal welfare ambassador.

As I followed the subtitles, I knew I had to go to Scotland and make my birthday wish come true. My future plans were starting to take shape.

The same year, Wu Hung and I got to know the International Association of Human–Animal Interaction Organizations (IAHAIO) and traveled to Geneva to attend the IAHAIO Conference, where we again made many new contacts. After the conference, we accepted invitations to visit Germany, Switzerland, and France. While we were in Strasbourg, Princess Elisabeth de Croÿ and Amelia Tarzi arranged for Wu Hung to address the European Parliament on the stray dog problem in Taiwan. Both ladies were familiar with the issue and had been following the development and progress of the Pet Respect campaign. Elisabeth was an advisory director of the WSPA and a well-known international animal welfare ambassador. Amelia was a member of the Geneva Animal Protection Society and an interpreter for conferences at the European Parliament and the United Nations. Both Elisabeth and Amelia had been to Taiwan with Joy at different times, Elisabeth as a guest of the government and Amelia as a presenter at the LCA's humane education conference for teachers.

Seeing that people in Europe cared about the plight of stray dogs in Taiwan was incredibly encouraging. It made me think that perhaps the world was not as vast as I had thought, and perhaps people had similar hopes and dreams after all, regardless of their race and culture, or where in the world they happened to live. In a relatively short time, I had been exposed to so many individuals and organizations in the US and Europe willing to discuss the various injustices afflicting humans and animals that needed international attention and support. I had been inspired and seen a new side of life. I was beginning to think that perhaps I had something to contribute to this global movement. I was beginning to get my muddled thoughts into some sort of order.

From France, Wu Hung and I traveled to the UK, staying at Joy's new home in London close to the WSPA office. She had moved in only the day before and had no furniture, but at least we had a roof over our heads, and we got some warmth from camping on the floor.

My next step was to prepare my family. Although we were never a tightly knit family after my mother's death, we still had a sense of duty toward each other. I was most nervous about telling my first sister, fearing she would become distressed and treat my departure as yet another loss. When I told my siblings that I was planning to leave Taiwan, they were all alarmed and worried about me, especially as I was unable to say whether I would ever return. Was I going away for a month, two or three months, or a year? Would we ever see each other again? I simply didn't know. My vague and noncommittal attitude added to my family's anxiety and concern as they remembered my unstable and often irrational thoughts and behavior in the past. I had little money, I didn't know where I would stay or end up in the long run, and I was traveling alone and could barely speak English. They were distressed.

On the other hand, my colleagues at the LCA, although initially surprised, were mostly supportive—especially Mr. Chang, the benefactor who provided our office space and my salary. Wu Hung, as always, listened carefully to my hopes and tentative plans and helped me prepare for my departure. The plan was that I would leave Taiwan in June 1996 with Wu Hung and LCA volunteers, who were going to Washington, DC, to attend an animal rights conference, then I would strike out on my own when they returned to Taiwan.

I tried to maintain a positive outlook, but I had anxieties of my own. How would I cope without Wu Hung to lean on? He had been my mentor, always so trustworthy and reliable, for so many years. Could I manage without him? As the weeks went by, I became physically drained—a nervous wreck—from worry and a lack of sleep.

2001. Wu Hung and EAST, his newly formed society protesting against bear farming, with a mechanical bear showing how bear bile is collected.

I was fearful of the unknown and uncertain of myself, almost self-loathing, and exhausted from incessant headaches. But I knew I had to leave my past and forge a new life in which I could feel useful to society, be confident, and do worthwhile work.

In the summer of 1996, I said goodbye to all that was familiar to me, having lived in Taiwan my whole life. It was such a wrench, and at times, I did wonder if I was having a mental and physical breakdown—if I was perhaps even on a path to self-destruction. But something inside me was telling me to leave. My sisters rallied in support as we said our goodbyes and thoughtfully gave me a credit card to use, knowing how little money I had.

As I traveled with Wu Hung and the volunteers from the LCA to Washington, DC, to attend the National Animal Rights Conference, I felt like a part of the LCA still and was able to push the uncertainty of the coming days to the back of my mind. At the conference, I enthusiastically joined in the protests we held in the streets, during

1996. Michael Kaufman at his farm in Colorado, showing Pei how to feed the newborn calf.

which we distributed postcards embossed with the message DOGS ARE NOT GARBAGE to passersby and asked them to send the cards to the Taiwanese government via the Taipei Representative Office. We joined the animal rights march and headed to Capitol Hill, where Wu Hung and Yu Min (the LCA's administrator) addressed the crowds from the stage.

After the street actions, followed by a sightseeing tour of New York, Wu Hung and the LCA volunteers returned to Taiwan. I was now on my own.

Before leaving Taiwan, I had arranged for my first destination to be Farm Sanctuary, an animal rescue operation on a 275-acre farm in upstate New York. Farm Sanctuary was established in 1986 by Gene Baur, an activist in the animal rights and food justice movements. I was to work there as an intern. During my internship, I shared a room with five other interns, all students from the nearby Cornell University and all American girls about ten years younger than me.

1996. Pei as an intern at Farm Sanctuary, Upstate New York.

The reality of my new life, without a familiar language, familiar faces or buildings, was daunting: I felt so alone and insecure. The first month was almost unbearable, but I had to put on a brave face. Being a city girl, I had never been to a farm before, yet here I was, deep in the countryside and feeling so cold even though it was summertime. The summer air here was indeed much different from the hot, humid atmosphere in Taiwan. And what a culture shock I experienced! Having never lived on my own, I cried every night. Once, I rang Wu Hung and nervously asked, "I think I have made a mistake, should I come back?" A very firm "NO" from the other end of the phone sealed my fate.

Despite being so homesick, I enjoyed contact with the animals. My duties varied: on some days, I was cleaning droppings out of the rabbit hut; on other days, I was feeding the goats and turkeys. I was wary of the unpredictable goats, as they would prance around butting anyone or anything in their path, but the turkeys were such

1996. Pei with the turkeys at Farm Sanctuary, Upstate New York.

lovely creatures. They were not timid like the chickens, and one turkey in particular loved having his neck stroked. The manager of the farm was an American-Korean lady who somehow sensed I was struggling and looked after me as best she could. Although she had her own work to do, she still found time to take me shopping on her day off, which I truly appreciated. I tried hard not to appear unhappy, and within a couple of weeks, I was starting to feel less apprehensive.

Besides feeding the animals and cleaning their living and sleeping quarters, I also worked as a chalet maid, served breakfast, worked in the gift shop, and sometimes took a group of people on a tour of the facilities. Given my very limited English, I had to memorize a script; I was very nervous, but being the occasional tour guide certainly helped boost my confidence.

When my month-long internship was completed, I moved on to stay with Michael Kaufman, Education Director of the American Humane Association (AHA), which had two main departments, Child Protection and Animal Protection. I had first met Michael at an IAHAIO event, where he had generously offered me a one-month internship at his home. I stayed with him and his husband Rick on their farm on the outskirts of Kiowa, Colorado, near Denver. The several acres of land on the farm housed numerous animals including chickens, fish, horses, rabbits, dogs, cats, sheep, and goats. Notwithstanding my previous internship at Farm Sanctuary, I was still new to farm work and was learning on the job, but I now felt more confident around animals and eagerly helped to feed them and clean their living quarters.

The highlight of my stay, without a doubt, was watching a Brown Swiss cow with white markings on her head give birth to a beautiful calf and then being asked to name the calf. I named her Zhong-ai, "First Love," for the love of a mother animal upon seeing her child for the first time. I watched as this helpless calf suddenly gained strength and took her wobbly, unsteady first steps, then as her mother nudged her gently into position so she could suckle for the first time. It was all like a miracle. As the calf's body started to dry, she emerged with a velvet-textured coat, lighter in color than her mother's, almost like milk coffee.

Any knowledge I had had about caring for animals prior to coming to the US was just theory gleaned from books, but I loved the practical work. It was all so new and exciting. I marveled especially at the gentleness of the large animals, the horses and the cows. Michael and Rick, ever so kind and patient, taught me how to be calm and confident when moving around the animals. It was one of the most memorable and engaging four weeks of my entire life.

Once I got over my initial panic from being alone, I told myself I was now following the path to my destiny. With this new attitude, I was able to enjoy a busy and enlightening three months in the US, visiting education organizations, government animal shelters, and zoos, and even attending a disaster relief training course, in which I learned how to rescue an animal from a body of water and get him or her into a boat.

From the US, I traveled to Sweden, Denmark, France, and Switzerland to learn from national organizations doing the same work as those I had visited in the US, only focusing on companion animals. I did a further internship with the Zurich Animal Protection Society, staying at its animal care center that was high up in the Black Forest, accessible only by cable car. On its way up, the cable car passed by grand houses nestled in the mountains that I was told were owned by movie stars and other well-known celebrities. Once at the center, I was struck by the marked contrast between this dedicated animal care facility, set against such a picturesque backdrop, and the dingy wire cages and pits for keeping stray dogs in Taiwan.

With some surprise and pride, I realized that I was now truly engaged with the global animal welfare movement. By the end of the summer, with work experience in the US and Europe under my belt, I was onto the next leg of my journey—this time onto London, where I planned to study sociology at university, focusing on social welfare and animal rights. But first, I needed to enroll at a language school as my reading and writing skills were still not adequate for formal studies.

I had arranged to stay at Joy's home again, but due to a communication breakdown, Joy was not expecting me until the following month. As it happened, when I arrived in the UK, she was in Australia, so I was instead greeted at London Heathrow by a very tall Englishman, who approached me and said: "Hello, I'm Brian. Joy has asked me to meet you. You are coming to stay with me." Tired from traveling and nervous about arriving in yet another country, I wasn't sure if I understood what he was saying. Without speaking, I meekly followed this stranger to his car and he started driving.

The journey seemed to take forever as the traffic was so congested, although coming from Taiwan, I should have been accustomed to heavy traffic and traffic jams. Brian chatted for most of the drive; I nodded along, yet I could not understand his soft accent, which I later learned was Scottish, diluted throughout his years of living in London. We arrived at Brian's house in Brixton to the sound of loud reggae music echoing through the streets and a pleasant smell of what I thought was perfume but later discovered was marijuana. I learned that Brixton was a popular destination for people from the Caribbean islands, many having settled here with their extended families and brought their culture with them. In the last fifty years, people of other origins had also settled in Brixton, transforming the area into a colorful melting pot of many nationalities.

Joy and Brian used to work together and regularly had visitors from other countries staying in their respective homes, so Brian and his partner Tim were very relaxed about their new Chinese housemate. They looked after me well, sensing that I was apprehensive about living in an unfamiliar country. I stayed with them until Joy returned from Australia. Tim was an active local politician and the mayor of Lambeth, the largest district in London, so Brian was always busy, either campaigning for Tim or organizing volunteers who distributed political leaflets in the nearby neighborhoods. They were both interested in other cultures, and during my stay, we discussed (as best we could given my limited English, with the help of my electronic translator) Taiwan's emerging democracy compared with the democratic process in the UK, one of the oldest democracies in the world.

Sadly, Tim later died from a terminal illness at only forty years of age. For the past twenty-five years, Brian has been a close friend of mine. He acted as my surrogate father and gave me away at my wedding some years after I arrived in the UK. Brian also became the first president of ACTAsia, the organization I would eventually start in 2006.

Once settled in Joy's home, I began to plan the next steps of my personal and professional development. Through all this, Buddhism was still a major part of my life. I was still in regular contact with Wu Hung and other Buddhist friends, and I set up a small shrine in Joy's sitting room where I practiced my devotion each day. Joy and Gitte, her Danish colleague who lived with us, may have found this rather unusual, but even if they did, they tolerated me and kept out of the way.

I enrolled in an English language course in London. Since it wasn't going to start for a couple of months, I arranged to gain some more work experience with Dogs Trust, the Royal Society for the Prevention of Cruelty to Animals (RSPCA), and the WSPA, all well-established NGOs. As in Taiwan, I discovered there were many stray and unwanted dogs and cats in the UK; here, however, they were not on the streets creating a commotion but were brought to shelters, either by owners unable to keep them or by the trained district council animal wardens who had caught them humanely. Unlike in Taiwan, where street dogs had historically been discarded as vermin and garbage, these animals were treated with respect and care, with dedicated staff for their rehoming.

I discovered numerous resources for shelter employees—for example, on animal handling, behavior, nutrition, and socialization—and I was fortunate enough to have the opportunity to go to Kyiv, Ukraine, and take part in the RSPCA's international animal welfare training course, which proved useful for me as the teaching was pitched at a basic level. Animal welfare advocacy was in its infancy in Eastern Europe at that time, and I could relate to the challenges there, such as the lack of a legal framework. It was only six years since the collapse of communism in Ukraine. Under the restrictive regime of the Soviet Union, keeping an animal as a pet had been considered frivolous and discouraged, but once they were free to make their own choices, many people in ex-Soviet countries were keen to have companion animals. New Ukrainian animal welfare groups were emerging that were in a situation much like my own, with only a limited understanding of animal welfare concepts.

But now that I was settled in London, my priority was to visit Scotland!

I loved every minute of the journey. The train raced from the south of England to the north through varied landscapes—flatlands at the beginning, then rolling countryside and villages, with fields covered in bright yellow flowers, whose seeds were used to make rapeseed oil, and ancient cathedrals towering above houses and shops. The border between England and Scotland was just two miles from Berwick, where twenty-eight arches carried the railway track high above the River Tweed. Finally, I arrived at my destination—Edinburgh, Scotland's capital city. I was there only for a few days, but just seeing the rugged landscape, hearing the music, and admiring the tartan clothes brought back the feelings I had experienced while watching the film *Braveheart*. I knew I had made the right choice to follow my destiny. (Some ten years later, I married Ross, a man with Scottish heritage, so he and the groomsmen wore kilts at our wedding. I have returned to Scotland many times in the past twenty-five years and on each occasion, I have felt the same tingling sensation—like I had returned to my spiritual home.)

It was now time for me to begin my English language course; I needed better English to find a job at some stage. Now back in London, I plunged into studying with some apprehension but also enthusiasm as I tried hard to master the pronunciation. Like many Chinese nationals, I struggled to correctly pronounce "r" and "v" sounds. The class had twelve students from different countries, and I became friendly with a man who was a refugee from Iran and now a resident student in Sweden. He was taking the course in the hope that it would help him in his future career as a chemical engineer. Our friendship grew as we practiced our pidgin English on each other; two lonely people in a foreign land with no family members to talk to in our own languages, two misfits, we drifted closer together. At the end of the course, in December 1996, he returned to Sweden to carry on with his university studies, but we kept our relationship alive.

Having set my heart on studying for a master's degree in sociology, I applied to numerous universities. Frustratingly, my qualifications from the college in Taipei were not accepted by the UK's admission system. I also approached an agent who helped students from overseas find universities that would take them, but as his fees were too high, I was unable to pay him. I kept applying anyway. Eventually, I was offered two choices, a diploma course in sociology at the University of Essex on its Colchester campus or a Master of Business Administration (MBA) program at the University of Kent. I consulted Mr. Chang, himself a successful businessman, on which option he thought would be best for me if I were to return to work in Taiwan. He advised me to study sociology as there were already lots of people in Taiwan with an MBA and having one would probably not improve my job prospects. I understood and heeded his advice, and accepted the University of Essex's offer to study for a diploma in sociology.

I set off for Colchester with just enough money to cover the tuition and accommodation fees for one term and little idea how I would be able to continue afterwards, although I had enrolled in a three-year course. I decided to just block this problem from my mind and take things one day at a time. I still had the credit card my sisters had given me for emergencies before I left Taiwan; they also regularly sent me parcels containing Chinese foods—packets of noodles, dried biscuits, vitamin powders, and the likes. *I should be able to survive*, I thought. I was allocated a newly built, comfortable albeit small room—well equipped, with cupboards and a desk—on the new campus. I shared a kitchen and laundry facilities with other students.

The diploma course was less demanding than I had expected, so I asked my supervisor if I could transfer to a master's program. He said that he himself had no objections but that it was not his decision: the department's academic committee had to agree, based on an assessment of my academic abilities and proficiency in the English language. To my great surprise and delight, the committee approved my request, and I immediately transferred to the higher-level course.

I could finally breathe a sigh of relief: now, I no longer had to worry about nine months' worth of tuition fees and living costs, as the master's course was just eighteen months in duration. Moreover, I had already done one term of the undergraduate course, so I was able to get credits toward my master's degree. The new course was far more demanding, and I studied for long hours, with little sleep and food. Often, late at night, I would fax questions and passages of text to Joy for her guidance. I can remember some very long faxes relating to my thesis that spanned several days, exchanged between us throughout the evening and well into the night. Joy was recovering from an illness and was not at work at the time, so she could catch up on sleep during the day, while I had to go to class.

Determined to successfully pass my course, I was obsessively studying at almost every waking moment. I rarely socialized, focusing only on my goal. I needed this qualification, which would give me credibility and widen my opportunities in the future. All of this studying took a toll. I became stressed and overly anxious, and my weight dropped to an alarming 38 kilograms. I felt weak, with constant headaches and a nauseous feeling most of the time. Then, one day, I developed a high fever and was admitted as an emergency to Colchester General Hospital. I was diagnosed with H influenzae meningitis, which left me weak and disoriented for a couple of weeks. After a period of recovery filled with good food, I returned to my studies, eventually receiving my Master of Arts in sociology.

Now, it was time for me to get a job and repay my sisters the money they had loaned me through the credit card. My first and second sisters were now running their own small boutique in Taipei, selling designer clothes, and my third sister was working for an export company. My brother had two sons, Ci Wei Lin and Wei Hsiang Lin, and was running a taxi service. All our lives had changed.

Since my departure from Taiwan, I had still remained in close contact with Wu Hung and the LCA. In fact, I was still involved with the LCA as its international representative, keeping the organization informed about developments in the animal welfare movement in Europe and regularly scouring publications and websites for any articles of interest. One day, Joy saw an advertisement placed by the RSPCA, looking for someone to join its international department. Dared I apply? I wasn't really confident, but Joy convinced me that there was nothing to lose. I applied and was invited to an interview. To my great surprise, I got the job. Elated, I immediately accepted. To my even greater surprise, only a few days later, I was offered another job by the CEO of the WSPA, this time as a project officer for Asia! How could I possibly choose between these two leading organizations?

The RSPCA, the oldest animal protection organization in the world, was established in England in 1824. When I was working with the LCA in Taiwan, I had collected some resources from the RSPCA to help me and my colleagues build our knowledge of animal welfare, never dreaming that I might one day be offered a job there.

Conflicting thoughts engulfed my mind. How would I cope with the formality of the RSPCA? Perhaps it was too British for me at this stage? The WSPA's London office had many non-British people working there, perhaps I would fit in better at the WSPA? In addition, by now, I had done some volunteer work at the WSPA and was familiar with the office and some of the staff. I knew Victor and Joy well as they had both worked with me in Taiwan, but neither of them tried to influence me, so I had to make my own decision. I knew it would be considered unprofessional to accept a job offer one day and then reject it a few days later, but at the time, I truly felt I was better suited to the WSPA, especially given its ongoing work in several Asian countries. But how could I withdraw my previous decision? I now faced the embarrassment of having to explain my change of heart to the RSPCA. Looking back, I think I was in awe of the RSPCA because of its long history, whereas being very much a novice at the time, I would be much more compatible with a more flexible organization. So, despite my admiration for the work of the RSPCA, after careful deliberation, I decided to accept the job with the WSPA.

What was happening to me was like a dream—I could hardly believe it. My mind was in a whirl. I had never really thought my concern for animal welfare could open up any sort of career path. I had just thought I would try to see as much as I could of the world and learn as much as I could about societies in which animals were not just things to be used and discarded when no longer needed. I hadn't given much thought to how long I would stay away from Taiwan. My sisters often asked me the same question, and I would always reply that I didn't know.

My work experience in the US and Europe and my university studies changed in my life. I was no longer a frustrated, lost soul, thinking the whole world was against me, but was gradually beginning to think more logically and long-term. I remember reflecting on my growth at the three-year mark of my time abroad: by then, I had improved my English, achieved a professional qualification, and now landed my dream job. I was gaining confidence; suddenly, life was looking good.

To work in the UK, I needed a work permit, which meant the WSPA would need to be my sponsor. The organization was willing to deal with all the legalities and the financial costs, but it would expect me to stay for an agreed-upon length of time. Confronted with a difficult decision, I now had to make my mind up. Did I want to live and work in the UK for at least the next three years? I decided I would stay. The WSPA started the visa application process as my sponsor, with January 1999 as the start date for my employment.

Throughout my time as a student at the University of Essex, my relationship with my former classmate and now-boyfriend from Iran had continued; we had met on occasion on weekends and during term holidays. He was aware I had accepted the WSPA's job offer. As I had to wait three months for my visa before I could work in the UK, I went to live with him in Sweden; on his part, he agreed to return to the UK, where we would live together, so I would be able to take up my position with the WSPA. With so much happening, we decided to add marriage to the mix; our wedding took place in France, just after I completed my studies.

We found an apartment to rent in south London and set up a home. But within only a few months, life became sour. Our cultures were too different. He was surprised to find that I was an independent woman who was not reliant on a man, unlike what he was accustomed to in his culture. He was not comfortable if I went out without him to accompany me; he expected to choose my friends and clothes, to make personal decisions on my behalf. He was suspicious and began to accuse me of encouraging who he thought were male friends, including professional contacts I had made in the US and Europe. He would turn up at my workplace if I was working late, checking to see that I was there. It was a distressing and eye-opening experience for me. I learned a costly lesson about cultural differences, which, in our case, rapidly created an unhealthy barrier between us that left me feeling more and more isolated as the days and weeks passed by. After two years, we went our separate ways.

I decided that for the foreseeable future, I would continue to live and work in the UK. I enjoyed my work and was eager to learn all I could and see where it would lead me. My sisters were disappointed that I was not returning to Taiwan but pleased that I had been offered not just one, but two job opportunities. My two eldest sisters were now both married, my first sister Mei Ling to Luis Yuan from South Korea, and my second sister Mei Jung to Wei Ming Huang, now with a baby daughter, Tzu-Chen Huang. My third sister Mei Ru, now known as Jessica Su, was living in China with her boyfriend Timmy Chuang and working for an export company that made Christmas ornaments. They later married and had a daughter, Nai Hui Chuang. So, in just a few years, my brother and sisters had all become settled in their jobs and were in stable relationships. Though not dependent on each other, we now felt closer spiritually and more united as a family.

Chapter 9

The WSPA Years

My first day working at the WSPA was in January 1999, and by the end of it, I was already beginning to feel like a fish out of water. Although I was a graduate of a university in the UK, with work experience in the US and Europe, I was not prepared for the work culture and fast-moving environment at the WSPA. Nervous, I could feel myself floundering, although I tried hard to disguise any hint of uncertainty. I was only too aware that my spoken English, with a strong Chinese accent, might be difficult for some people to understand and that my written English was not that good either. Would I really be able to master the job? I was apprehensive.

Physically, the WSPA's office was awe-inspiring enough; even its location was like something out of a British film. Our office was on the fourteenth floor of a fifteen-story 1960s square-shaped building on the banks of the River Thames. Although the building was plain and ordinary in design, it had large windows on all four sides, so the views from inside the open-plan office were spectacular, with miles of London, including its famous landmarks and river bridges, visible. The office directly overlooked the Houses of Parliament, the Tate Gallery, and MI5, the government agency responsible for internal security and counterterrorism.

Even more intimidating were our immediate neighbors, as we were sandwiched between the building that housed the Flying Squad, the elite undercover anti-robbery unit of the Metropolitan Police, and the building known as MI6, the UK government's foreign secret intelligence service. Well-known fictional British secret agent James Bond works for MI6 under the codename 007, and in many scenes of the James Bond films that include the MI6 building, the less impressive WSPA building can be seen alongside or in the background.

The workday here was so different from what I'd known in Taiwan, where the workplace was a serious environment with no time for chitchat. To my surprise, staff at the WSPA would speak with each other intermittently throughout the day and at times laugh out loud, seeming too relaxed to be at work. Even more surprising to me, though, was that the CEO was just as relaxed. At the time, I was using my full name, Pei Feng, which, when pronounced by English speakers, sounded similar to "Pay Fern." But since he was a Scot and never managed to pronounce it correctly, to him, I was "Pay Phone." He would call out to me, "Hi Pay Phone, everything OK?" But before I could respond, he was asking someone else the same thing.

In Taiwan, we never asked anyone, "How are you?" or, "Everything OK?" unless we needed to start a conversation, so at first, if someone at work said to me, "How are you?" I would start to explain. It took me some time to understand that this was usually just a throwaway pleasantry and that if someone really wanted to know how I was, they would engage further. As I became more confident, I complained that work could not get done when people seemed to spend so much time chatting. I compared my new working life with my former one in Taiwan, where the office was usually silent. Breaks for morning coffee, lunch, and afternoon tea, in addition to as many personal breaks as one wanted, and regular working hours were almost nonexistent at the LCA. People knew they must start early and stay until the work was done, only stopping for a few minutes to eat, while seated at their desks if necessary. I was mystified that our WSPA office would become deserted around midday, with some people drifting off to the pub, returning for a few hours in the afternoon, then leaving for the pub again around 5 p.m. "Why do English people need to go to the pub so often?" I queried. In Taiwan, it was far more common for people to have a meal together than to go out just to drink, but even then, rarely during working hours.

Over time, I began to understand that there were significant differences between social interactions in Taiwan and those in the UK. I realized that having been brought up in a non-democratic country, I was programmed to accept what I was told to do and how I was told I should act. What was considered discussion in the UK was instead chitchat in Taiwan, which was discouraged in our culture, and gossip in Buddhist teachings. Now, I was in a work environment where employees were encouraged to give their opinions and suggestions and plan much of their own workday, so if continuing their discussions with a colleague or thinking through difficult problems in a non-work environment such as a nearby café or a pub was useful, then it was acceptable.

I tried to get used to office chatter, but I still rarely joined in and, on occasion, felt intimidated by the raucous laughter of male colleagues. One day, my line manager said she had received complaints about me. Some colleagues thought I was rude, complaining that I tended to ignore them and did not thank them when they had done something to help me. "Why do I need to speak to them and thank them when they are here to do a job?" was my response. Sometimes, at lunchtime, colleagues asked me along to the cafeteria, located on the ground floor of our building, but why would I want to go there? I couldn't eat the food. All that were available for vegetarians were cold sandwiches made up of lettuce, cheese, and bread, which my colleagues enjoyed, but the type of food I was used to and yearned for was hot and more liquid, such as noodles. I found it difficult to swallow bread and cold fillings, and whenever I tried, I felt as if I would vomit.

Although there were several other foreigners of different nationalities working in the office, they all seemed to fit in, so why did I feel like a misfit? I kept telling myself that it was because I was the first Chinese person to work in the animal welfare sector in Europe. My colleagues were probably not comfortable around me because I was used to a different way of thinking and behaving from theirs. I was a square peg in a round hole, so to speak. I felt out of my depth. How could I overcome this situation?

Things started to change after I responded to a newspaper advertisement. An elderly man who was learning Mandarin and studying Taoism and Buddhism was looking for a Chinese person to help him improve his conversational Mandarin and understand Chinese culture. In exchange, he would help the Chinese person improve their English and learn about British culture. I eagerly applied, and shortly after, our mutually beneficial lessons began.

My new tutor-cum-student was of great help to me. I learned that "how are you" tended to be just a friendly acknowledgment, so the expected answer was usually "fine, thank you." I told him of my difficulties in the workplace, and he explained to me that I had to change the way I worked and fit in with the British nine-to-five work culture. If I was always staying late at work and not taking breaks, that might make some colleagues feel uncomfortable and might even be viewed by others as me showing off. Importantly, I needed to learn how to be a team player.

I realized that in contrast to my early impression of WSPA staff as lazy and noisy, they were extremely hardworking and amiable employees who produced professional results and supported their colleagues. I gradually started to make friends with some of them and learn how to work as part of a team. It was hard to change my way of thinking and my way of working; despite my best efforts, I was unhappy for some time. I watched with envy how quickly other new employees seemed to fit in; however, none were Asian, other than Deepa Balaram, who was Indian but had lived in Europe and worked in the UK for several years. (Some six years later, Deepa became the co-founder of ACTAsia.)

After a few months, I was becoming more familiar with the work environment at the WSPA and getting to know my colleagues. I was working closely with Victor, and we planned several investigations relating to wild animals in captivity. In many ways, for me, working with Victor was like working with Wu Hung back at the LCA in Taiwan, both of them being unassuming and kindly individuals. A zoologist, Victor was already an authority on wild animals, both in the wild and in captivity, and during his long career at the WSPA, he had become an experienced and successful investigator. In comparison, I was just an enthusiastic amateur at the time, but over the next few years, I would gain confidence and develop expertise in the arts of cunning and disguise.

My job title at the WSPA was Project Officer and my role was to liaise with the WSPA's network of member societies—350 animal protection groups in countries around the world. I was tasked with finding out how the WSPA could best help the Asian member societies with their respective work by providing practical support, appropriate resources, and relevant information. This opened up a wonderful opportunity for me to learn about how people in different countries understood and worked to promote animal welfare.

In particular, whenever I got to visit developing countries, such as Indonesia, the Philippines, and India, where poverty dominated so many people's lives, it was humbling to see how even people who had very little shared what they had with each other while caring for the animals they relied on for their livelihood—animals such as goats, chickens, donkeys, buffalo, and camels. Although my own family had lived mainly hand to mouth when I was a child, we lived in the city, so we still experienced far fewer hardships compared to for those living in rural communities, sometimes without water and electricity. Such communities, I found, had an understanding of the well-being of their animals and compassion for their animals, even if the animals were mainly kept to provide food.

Most of the WSPA's member societies were small in size and lacking in resources, with just one or two key people plus volunteers, who ran animal shelters (often using their own money) or lobbied for change through legislation. In contrast, the few older, more established member societies in developed countries had spacious offices and salaried staff, including marketing teams to raise public awareness and secure support for their work.

Looking back, I think what I gained intellectually from the member societies by experiencing their traditions and cultures far outweighed the limited practical help I was able to give to them.

Nevertheless, one area of my work where I felt comfortable and confident involved the creation of an Asian network, which we named AsiaLink, in the year 2000. It consisted of representatives from member societies in twelve countries—Bangladesh, China, India, Indonesia, Japan, Korea, Malaysia, Nepal, Philippines, Singapore, Sri Lanka, and Thailand. AsiaLink was the first international Asian network to be set up that focused on animal welfare and humane education. We provided resources, materials, knowledge, and small project grants to groups within the network, thereby introducing the term "capacity building," and facilitated combined efforts among them, with these groups working together as an alliance. Today, there are many other initiatives within the animal welfare movement in Asia to support capacity building, such as online courses and regular conferences—spaces for sharing knowledge and expertise.

1999. Pei visiting a municipality clinic in Jaipur where the animal birth control program was done in cooperation with Help in Suffering.

In 1993, the World Health Organization (WHO), in collaboration with the WSPA, had published *The Management and Control of Stray and Unwanted Dogs*, containing recommendations for governments and municipalities on humane methods of stray animal control. At the time, the WSPA was encouraging member societies to introduce spaying and neutering as a means to ultimately reduce street dog populations, and one of the first member societies to take on this challenge was Help in Suffering (HIS) in Jaipur, India. Once I was working for the WSPA, my first member society visit was to India to assess how HIS's work was progressing. The organization was and continues to be well-run, championing the WHO-WSPA recommendations at their animal birth control hospital. Back in the 1990s, the countless stray dogs and puppies on the streets of Jaipur represented a potential rabies threat, so if a person was attacked or bitten, the municipality would collect and dispose of the dogs, often by inhumane methods. The WSPA assisted HIS in setting up a clinic to catch, vaccinate, and spay or neuter dogs, then release them back to the streets. Jack Reece, a young vet from the UK, was sent there to help train local vets. Now, more than twenty-five years later, Jack is still involved with HIS in Jaipur.

I traveled to India with Ray Butcher, one of the WSPA's consultant veterinarians who was assessing the project and advising on some of the inevitable animal health issues, such as skin problems, distemper, and untreated injuries. Ray was a most amusing man, always joking except while on the job, when he transformed into the perfect professional and a great teacher. I learned a lot from him about animal behavior and management during that visit.

1999. Jaipur, the Pink City.

As we drove around Jaipur, the capital city of the state of Rajasthan, I was overwhelmed by the sheer number of magnificent temples, fortresses, and majestic palaces, most of them painted in a pink terracotta color, resulting in Jaipur's popular name, the Pink City. The overall effect was simply spectacular. But amid such beauty, there were so many beggars—people with deformities, elderly people, children, and young women with babies in their arms, all pleading for any offering. In addition, many animals were wandering around—cows, pigs, monkeys, dogs, and cats, foraging and snuffling for food or weaving in and out of the traffic, oblivious to the chaos from thronging crowds and the noise from hooting vehicles. Most of the animals were emaciated, with obvious, untreated wounds and diseases.

I had never seen beggars on the streets in Taiwan or China as vagrancy was forbidden by law, and I had never seen loose cows or pigs on the streets in busy cities. The visit to India was educational: I was experiencing yet another culture, so different from my own and also so different from those of the US and the UK. I wondered just how many different cultures there were in the world. I found India to be a country of many disparities, with extreme wealth and extreme poverty seeming to exist almost side by side. But was I making assumptions? After all, I had been to only one state in India. I reminded myself that India had one of the largest populations in the world (the figure is now 1.4 billion) and that each state was like a country unto itself. I needed to keep an open mind and not make judgments on scant information.

Following our trip to India, Ray, who had become a good friend and mentor, invited me to his veterinary clinic in Essex to see how the day-to-day operations of his clinic were run. At the premises, I was fascinated by the waiting room, which was decorated in cheerful colors and well stocked with free information leaflets for owners to take away. It even had a crèche with animal-themed murals and toys for small children to enjoy while waiting with their parents. It was more like an education center or a library than a waiting room, in stark contrast to the cold, impersonal veterinary clinics in Taiwan. I remembered Joy's comment on one of her visits to Taiwan: "Why are the veterinary clinics on upper floors and why do owners have to carry or drag their animals up so many steps? The animals and owners look so distressed!" My answer then had been: "The higher floors are less expensive to rent, and no one thinks about the feelings of an animal or his owner. It's all about profit." Unlike in the US and the UK, there was little understanding of animal sentience and little empathy with animals, even within the veterinary profession. Years later, when I was finally able to introduce veterinary training education in China, compassion and empathy were integral principles underlying all our training courses.

2000. An investigation into the illegal turtle trade.

Chapter 10

INVESTIGATIONS

Looking back on my early life, I find it hard to describe my character as I can't recall any periods when I felt happy and secure for any length of time. This does not mean that I was desperately unhappy all the time, but more often than not, I tended to be anxious and apprehensive, fearing that something unpleasant was lurking around the corner. Through years of practice, I was an expert at keeping my true feelings well hidden, though. I now wonder what my school friends thought of me. To them, was I friendly, easily led, or simply confused and unhappy? One thing is for sure: I wasn't a leader as I lacked confidence and self-esteem.

In my late teens, I still probably didn't seem like someone with a particularly engaging personality to my classmates in college. I tended to be withdrawn, on the inside crying for the mother I had recently lost. I was indifferent about life in general, and at times, I envied other teenagers who had parents and stable home lives. To me, life seemed so unfair. Continuing to hide my emotions, I got on reasonably well with most of my classmates, however, and drifted along from day to day without any major drama.

Thankfully, I did have one loyal friend, Sarah, whom I've mentioned in previous chapters. She was with me when we both studied commerce at Business College, also at the Buddhist evening classes, and later when we volunteered at the LCA. Despite our very different backgrounds, she has always been a wonderful friend and source of support, and to this day, we are still close friends. When I was in college, we were required to write personal statements, but I didn't know what to write in the section about hobbies as I didn't have any. Given my family background, extracurricular classes in music, art, or gymnastics, which had to be paid for, were simply out of the question. I did like singing and dancing, occasionally daydreaming about either becoming a ballet dancer or joining a modern dance troupe, but as I had never had any training, it remained just a fleeting fancy.

In college, I wasn't interested in the cooking or knitting classes but decided to join the drama club to learn about acting and stage makeup, costumes, and lighting. I also joined the photography club, not because I was interested at first, but because Sarah was joining. She could afford to buy fancy cameras and equipment, which she willingly shared with me. I was eager to tag along to the photography classes with her. Also, there were more boys than girls at this club, so that was a bonus! How was I to know that years later, photography and acting skills would be most useful for my work with the WSPA, conducting covert investigations in many different countries?

My main college course was in business management, which included how to manage secretarial tasks and how to do efficient desk research. In the early 1990s, with no internet or email system, knowing how to collect information from publications or by telephone and fax was an exceedingly useful skill. We had to be resourceful, as media openness and freedom of information were almost nonexistent in Asia. This does still apply today but to a lesser extent, thanks to the internet and social media. Once I started to develop administrative skills, I could methodically catalog relevant information, which helped my work with the LCA tremendously. Since there was little understanding and expertise in Taiwan with regard to the topics we were researching—human rights, animal welfare, and environmental concerns—we spent hours trawling through publications sourced from international NGOs and learned as we went along.

1999. The barge crossing the river to the Bear Farm.

I now believe that some unexplained force was with me throughout my earlier life, preparing me for what lay ahead, as so much of what I had learned during my "wilderness" days eventually helped me face and ultimately overcome numerous challenges in later years. The LCA was a disciplined and structured organization, and we applied a basic formula to all of our projects: desk research, field investigation, analysis, action plan, implementation, monitoring, and evaluation. Now, in the twenty-first century, we have the added benefit of technology, which allows us to easily google just about anything and plan our fieldwork, mapping out escape routes. Technology gives early warnings of hazards such as bad weather conditions, landslides, and typhoons, giving us time to adjust prepared plans. Even so, many useful lessons I learned at the LCA in the pre-technology days have stayed with me and are still relevant to ACTAsia's operational work in the field, with one instance involving an unexpected bout of altitude sickness in Mongolia that affected most of our team.

1999. A bear in a typical small cage at the Bear Farm.

I have been involved in many covert investigations in my career, but one that stays foremost on my mind is our investigation of bear farms in China in 1999. I was working on the WSPA's main campaign Libearty, which focused on the abuse of bears worldwide. Working with Victor, I was already investigating the bear parks in Japan where sun bears were forced to perform tricks, such as bicycle riding, for tourists. Our other investigations shone light on bear baiting in Pakistan (with Asiatic black or brown bears forced to fight dogs while people gambled on the outcome), as well as on dancing bears in India, Greece, and Turkey (the bears being trained to "dance," then paraded around tourist areas to perform for money). (The training involves forcing a bear cub to stand on a piece of burning-hot tin, while the handler plays music on a violin or similar instrument. The intense pain causes the cub to lift his feet in jerking movements. Once conditioned this way, the bear would grow up associating the music with pain and start to "dance" to it.)

With these other bear projects underway, the WSPA planned to investigate the farms in China where bears were held in captivity and "milked"—had bile extracted from their gallbladders—once or twice a day. (Bile is a fluid necessary for the digestive process, produced in the gallbladder.) In 1984, commercial bear farms were established in China, keeping mainly Asiatic black bears for bear gallbladders, bear bile, and other body parts used to produce TCM. (There are three species of bear native to China: the brown bear, the Asiatic black bear, and the sun bear.) The use of bear parts for TCM can be traced back three thousand years, when bears were hunted in the wild and killed for their gallbladders. It was widely believed that these body parts had numerous benefits for the health and well-being of people, such as protecting the liver, curing hepatitis, improving eyesight, and

1999. Bear bile being strained.

reducing fever and inflammation. This belief is still alive today, even though there is no scientific evidence to support it, and the marketing of TCM continues to be successful, with ever-increasing demand for bear bile for use as an ingredient in shampoos, wine, eye drops, and ointments. During the recent COVID-19 pandemic, bear bile was even given to hospitals as a cure for the virus.

When the bear farms were set up, commercial farming was a new venture, not a traditional business. It was projected that a bear kept on a farm and milked for five years would produce a total amount of bile equivalent to that of 220 bears poached from the wild combined, so some claimed that the industry was protecting wild bears. However, evidence shows that most farms bought bears taken from the wild. Also, the same farms were taking bear cubs from their mothers at three months of age and training them to perform tricks, such as tightrope walking, or to fight each other in boxing matches for the amusement of visitors. Bear farms are legal in China and approved by the state and provincial authorities, but until the early 1990s, they were not made widely known to the public, in China or overseas. Once information started to leak and reach international animal welfare groups, there was widespread criticism of the cruelty involved in the industry and the suffering it inflicted.

Bears started to be milked for bile at around three years of age. They were moved into small cages suspended above the ground, thus being forced to lie squashed on metal bars, and fed a poor diet of mashed corn with apples, tomatoes, and sugar. Bile was extracted from them twice a day, during feeding time, via a catheter permanently inserted into their gallbladders. We knew that some bears lived like this for up to ten years, many with inflammation and painful sores around the catheter's point of exit, while others died before then from related illnesses such as internal abscesses, peritonitis, and septicaemia. Yet bears living free in the wild could reach thirty years of age.

1999. Products for sale at the Bear Farm shop.

The purpose of the WSPA investigation in 1999 was to determine the scale of the bear bile trade in China, its influence on and supply to the global market, and the animal welfare implications. It was decided that I, a Chinese person, should lead the investigation team, with two of my former colleagues from the LCA in Taiwan accompanying me. By this time, I had been working at the WSPA for almost a year and had even been promoted to Project Manager. I was becoming a more experienced investigator, having also developed an outline plan of action that could be applied to all investigations—a comprehensive strategy with room for modifications if needed.

Before we could embark on an investigation, there was a lot of background research to be done, as bear farms were difficult to find and usually located in remote areas in rural northern and western China. There were no Google maps in those days, so we searched for bear farms in the business section of telephone directories, then plotted their locations on a physical map. International animal welfare groups were learning how TCM was produced and were openly criticizing the bear bile industry for the extreme suffering caused to the animals. It was unlikely that bear farmers were aware of this criticism, given that there was no freedom of information in China, but it was still wise of us to avoid any unnecessary risks, especially as one of the bear farms had been exposed by foreigners. More foreigners (who were already a rare sight in these parts) asking questions about these farms would certainly arouse suspicion. So, when preparing for our investigation, the three of us, being Chinese-Taiwanese nationals, thought it unlikely we would look suspicious, although we were ever mindful of potential risks and the need to be careful.

China was starting to market the bear farms to its tourism industry, so we knew some of the larger farms were open to visitors. We decided to present ourselves as representatives of a TCM company from Taiwan, who were looking for business opportunities and were visiting to assess the viability of setting up a bear farm in Taiwan. We prepared business cards with fake names and contact details and thoroughly rehearsed our story in case we became separated and were closely questioned by employees at the farms. We also planned to disguise our appearances as best we could by wearing plain-glass spectacles and close-fitting hats.

We agreed that my colleagues would be using conventional cameras and I would use a covert pinhole camera. I had to memorize exactly where the covert pinhole camera would be positioned on my rucksack and how I needed to position my body in order to film the bears and facilities. It was important to get this right, as the film footage taken by pinhole cameras in those days was not as clear and detailed as footage from the more advanced covert cameras used today. Also, it was essential that we keep the camera equipment warm; otherwise, the batteries would not work, especially in areas close to the Russian and North Korean borders, where the weather would be icy cold. Making our travel arrangements was a complex process, as we planned on visiting as many as eleven bear farms in six provinces, all widely scattered throughout the southeast, southwest, and northeast regions, the major areas of the bear-farming industry.

China being a vast country, we would need to travel by plane, bus, and taxi, and also hire private drivers to take us to places where there was no other form of transport. Traveling in remote areas of China could be dangerous, due to not just the terrain, with rocky and muddy mountain slides, but also the risk of encountering robbers. In addition, if we were suspected of spying on a legal government activity with the intention of global exposure, we could be held in prison indefinitely, without our families or contacts being informed, so it would seem as if we had simply disappeared. No matter how much experience I had under my belt, I always felt apprehensive before starting an undercover investigation, thinking of all that could go wrong and reminding myself that thinking, responding, and moving quickly were vital to my safety. My daily meditation practice was of tremendous help in keeping me calm and resilient.

During our investigation, one of the bear farm visits seemed doomed before we even got to our overnight accommodation, where we were going to get ready to go to the farm the following morning. We had flown from our previous destination and were now heading for the North Korean border on a rickety minibus designed for fifteen people. The four-hour journey along winding country roads in extreme weather conditions was treacherous; exhausted after many grueling days of travel, I eventually fell asleep. When I awoke, I was alarmed to see the minibus overcrowded, with probably twice as many people as was permitted; while I was asleep, it had stopped to pick up people stranded along the road. Soon after, the driver stopped to pick up yet another passenger, a man who had fallen on the ice, with a large bump and gash on his head. Looking out of the window, I saw that the vehicle, which was not fitted with snow chains, seemed to be engulfed in a thick blanket of snow and was skidding and spinning on the icy road. With only the morbid thought that if we had an accident, we would not be found and would be entombed in ice and snow for our final resting place, I closed my eyes and prayed.

By a stroke of luck, we survived the ordeal. The next morning, after a short night's sleep in very basic accommodation, we continued our journey by taxi, stopping by a bear bile shop in another city. The spacious showroom, which was in a smart area of the city, had an impressive display of gallbladders and products made from bear bile, all lined up on glass shelves. We introduced ourselves to the shop owner as potential investors from Taiwan, and after a pleasant exchange of information about the bear bile industry and the range of products on sale, he offered to show us his bear farm, which was in a city suburb. We readily accepted. The shop owner arranged for a car to collect us the next morning.

When our transport arrived, my feelings of anticipation turned into horror as I saw the word COURT painted in large letters on the car. The driver explained that he worked for the court and used the car to earn extra cash. Still, we were too afraid to get in the car, thinking he might be lying. Was he doing something illegal? Was this a trap? Were we suspected of being spies? Feeling uneasy, I quickly made up a story that we had already hired a taxi to take us to the farm and that it would arrive shortly. Right away, I called for a taxi, and when it eventually arrived, we followed the court car.

After about thirty minutes of driving, the court car stopped alongside a river, and we were told by a person who had been waiting for us to get out of the taxi and take a barge to the farm. As soon as we were out of the taxi, it quickly sped away. Again, alarm bells were ringing in my head. We had no idea where we were going, or even where we were. We had to think quickly: if we didn't get on the barge and go through with our plan, we risked arousing suspicion;

plus, how would we get back with no vehicle? On balance, it seemed safer to calmly go ahead and visit the farm. After crossing the river, we followed our host on foot for about one mile, passing through a busy market where produce and household goods were sold—fruit and vegetables along with brooms and buckets.

Finally, we got to the bear farm. As we approached the large warehouse-type barns, we heard rumbling noises and the moaning of animals getting louder and louder. Upon entering, we saw long rows of cages housing Asiatic bears, the poor animals pacing and moaning nonstop. The bears barely had room to turn around in their small cages, which each measured about one by one by two meters. As we walked along the rows of cages, I could see that some of the bears had been declawed and had their teeth filed down; many were rocking their heads and bodies or biting the bars of their cages in desperation. We had to fake enthusiasm and admiration for what was in front of us, although on the inside, we were crying.

We steeled ourselves to watch bile being extracted from some of the bears. It took about one hour to milk a bear, and this was done twice each day. One of the bears whom I was standing close to looked directly at me, then with difficulty heaved his large body within his tiny cage, and I saw a large, weeping bald patch on his lower back that I would not have noticed had he not turned around. It was as if he were silently telling me about his suffering. (For months after this visit, whenever I closed my eyes, I could see this beautiful bear's eyes appealing to me.) We were shown how some of the bear bile was baked into crystals, an oven being used to dry the dark brown-green liquid. The crystals were then crushed and mixed with other ingredients such as rice wine to make infused liquors, to be sold as elixirs in pharmaceutical shops.

Having been filming covertly as well as openly all this time, we decided it was time to leave and walked back to the barge with the bear farm owner. Just after boarding the barge, suddenly, the owner's manner and tone of voice changed. Mild-mannered and friendly just a few minutes ago, he now started screaming at us, his face distorted in rage. He accused us of being reporters intending to do an exposé in Taiwan on his farm and demanded to see our identifications and empty the film from our cameras. Though terrified, we knew that when confronting an angry person, we should always stay calm and speak quietly. We faked expressions of bewilderment in response to his accusations, then meekly gave him the film and willingly showed him our (false) business cards. Eventually, he calmed down, though seemingly not convinced, and allowed us to go by barge back to the mainland. Thankfully, we still had the film taken by the pinhole camera.

We had no idea why his attitude toward us changed. Had one of us, without thinking, said something to arouse his suspicion, or perhaps revealed something through body language or facial expression? The incident was a sharp reminder that when investigating, we should never become complacent and always beware of potential danger.

During our visits to eleven farms in different parts of China, we saw several thousands of bears in confinement, exploited daily to meet the demand for bear bile. As a bear got older and no longer met the production quota, he was killed, his bladder and paws sold as delicacies. Today, more than twenty years after our investigation, bear farms are still thriving. Thanks to international pressure, the Chinese government did close some of the old, dilapidated farms where just a few bears were kept, and it agreed for those bears to be moved to the Animals Asia Foundation rescue center in Chengdu, Sichuan Province, in southwest China—a semi-natural sanctuary built for bears "retired" from the industry, so that they could live out their days free of pain and exploitation. However, this step in the right direction did not stop the government from building new facilities for housing more bears and expanding the trade in China. A typical large farm has between 500 and 3,000 bears, with an expansive, glossy showroom selling products such as bear-bile tincture, wine, capsules, moisturizing cream, and shampoo.

My knowledge of the way in which bears were farmed and milked for their bile led to my key role in further investigations into the extent of the national and international trades of items containing bear bile, such as shampoo, tea, wine, skin lotions, eye drops, and tonics. Bear parts such as paws and gallbladders were also in demand for medicinal use, and even wild bears were known to be killed to meet this demand. There was evidence contrary to China's claim at the time that it was not exporting bear parts or products containing bear bile and gallbladder out of mainland China, as the three bear species in China (the Asiatic black bear, Asian brown bear, and Malayan sun bear) were listed in the international Convention on International Trade in Endangered Species (CITES)—a global agreement between governments to protect wild flora and fauna. Ironically, China signed the CITES treaty in 1981.

We suspected that the international trade in bear bile and bear parts was still happening, so my next task was to liaise with the WSPA's AsiaLink member societies and design a comprehensive plan to survey pharmacies and TCM shops in Malaysia, Japan, Indonesia, Singapore, Thailand, Taiwan, the Netherlands, Canada, the US, Australia, and New Zealand. These investigations spanned a three-year period, with illegal products found to be on sale at international airports in China and in TCM shops in all of the countries above. The extent of the bear-product market in some countries clearly indicated there were well-established illegal channels to import and distribute large quantities. These products were also likely smuggled into countries by individuals for personal use or for friends and relatives. This extensive investigation that I have briefly outlined is fully detailed in the WSPA's 2002 publication *The Bear Bile Business: The Global Trade in Bear Products from China to Asia and Beyond.*

2002. Cage of dogs on sale at a market in Korea for human consumption.

Every day, there are so many animals suffering in so many different situations—in zoos, circuses, intensive farms, slaughterhouses, laboratories, and domestic settings. In 2001–2002, I traveled with Rob Laidlaw to Indonesia to investigate how wild animals in captivity were kept and trained to perform in circuses or exploited in other ways for entertainment. (Rob is the Founder and Executive Director of Zoocheck Canada, a chartered biologist, and an award-winning author of numerous children's books on animal welfare and wildlife protection.) We witnessed a young elephant being repeatedly bitten on the ear by his trainer as a way to get him to perform circus acts, at the same time as three other trainers were beating another young elephant who was howling and urinating out of intense terror. I could not stop the tears streaming from my eyes as I filmed such appalling treatment of such gentle creatures. On other occasions, while traveling and working with the WSPA's AsiaLink groups in their respective countries, I saw animals in zoos who were just skin and bones, close to death from malnutrition; hundreds of sea turtles stacked on top of each other in a cramped indoor pool, where they were kept to be killed for turtle satay; dogs, cats, and raccoons in small, piled-up cages in Asian markets, to be brutally killed at the point of sale so that their meat could be eaten while fresh; pigs and cows killed without any form of effective sedation in slaughterhouses. The list of cruelties and injustices seems endless.

Do these investigations stay in my mind, or have I been able to forget them? Whenever I've seen acts of violence toward humans or animals, in real life or on television, those images have stayed with me, but I have now learned to channel my thinking and use the same images and memories as motivation to work toward the day when vulnerable beings, human and nonhuman, will be treated with care and respect. Every minute, somewhere in the world, animals are being sacrificed for food, fashion, vanity, or the supposed medicinal benefits of their parts—benefits that have already been scientifically disproved.

I want to continue being a part of a movement that highlights these atrocities and contributes to a compassionate future. Up until this point, my focus had mainly been on animal welfare, but I was determined to one day develop a holistic approach to welfare that would be equally inclusive of people, animals, and the environment.

Despite rocky beginnings at the WSPA, I grew to love working there. I now realize that the organization was a wonderful training ground for me, giving me the opportunity to get to know many people in many countries, who all had a hand in my development within the animal welfare sector. I learned and grew from their examples and from the sheer diversity of my working life, as rarely were two workdays ever the same. After I left the WSPA after five years to set up ACTAsia for Animals, many of my former colleagues continued to help me by either volunteering or allowing me to adapt their materials for use in China.

Chapter 11

The Birth of ACTAsia: The First Five Years

By 2001, I was earning a good salary at the WSPA; I had even saved enough money to use as a deposit for a small, terraced house in one of the less fashionable areas of London. Buying a house seemed like the logical next step since I was planning on staying in the UK for the immediate future, so I set my sights on finding a house with a living room, a kitchen, a bathroom, two bedrooms, and a garden. It didn't occur to me that this might be a step too far for a young, single Asian woman, as most single women living in London preferred to rent an apartment or share a house with others, for reasons of safety, companionship, or affordability. London, like most other large cities around the world, had a significant incidence of crime, especially in the less favorable areas, but I was undeterred, determined to find what I wanted. I started house hunting, treating it as a major project.

Being able to afford to live only in certain areas of London, I went from house to house within my limited price range without finding anything suitable, as many of the houses were either in poor structural condition or located in unappealing neighborhoods, where petty theft and house break-ins were regular happenings. Then, by good fortune, I happened to view a typical Victorian terraced house in South London, owned by a Jamaican lady, that matched my requirements: two living rooms and a kitchen on the ground floor, and two bedrooms and a bathroom on the upper floor. And to my great surprise and delight, it had a garden, quite unusual in inner London.

Colorful like its owner, the house was decorated in vivid red, orange, yellow, green, blue, indigo, and violet—all the colors of the rainbow and more besides. The walls in all rooms either were painted in dazzling colors or featured patterned wallpaper, and large, multi-patterned curtains framed the windows. The house was well maintained and in good order throughout, so after a couple of visits to make sure it was the one for me, I agreed to buy it. There was even a historical feature in the garden—the remains of a World War II air-raid shelter. How exciting!

I wanted the house but could not secure the mortgage without putting down a larger deposit, so I turned to my second sister for help. By now, her fashion boutique was doing well and she had bought the premises in which it was located. To help me, she willingly mortgaged her shop to raise the balance of the money I needed to buy the house in South London. I was thrilled and beyond thankful for her generous and kind act. I agreed to repay her in regular monthly installments—as much as I could afford. I also had to repay the mortgage to the bank. Once again, I was on a tight budget, but I made it stretch to cover my living expenses, thanks to my new credit card.

I soon found some tradesmen to strip the walls of their various colors and repaint the house's interior in a neutral color scheme. I was living on my own for the first time in my life, and I had found a sanctuary. My sisters visited me from Taiwan and were so happy and proud to see that I not only had a job I loved but also had my own home. How my fortunes had changed in just five years! We had a lovely holiday together traveling around Europe, one of our most memorable stops being the picturesque, fragrant lavender fields in

Provence, France. I felt closer to my family than ever before. Back in Taiwan, my sisters were also happy and enjoying good fortune, running their fashion boutique together and enjoying the company of Mei Jung's little girl Chu Chu. My brother and his wife were similarly prosperous and content, living in a new home with their two boys and running their successful taxi business.

In 2003, I was promoted to the WSPA's Member Societies Director. Although I was proud and glad to get this promotion at first, I gradually realized that my role in the organization was changing. We had a new CEO, with different ideas and plans for the WSPA. The organization was changing direction, and I was expected to mobilize member societies to do campaigns on issues such as farming and whaling. Most of the member societies I was working with were run mainly by part-time volunteers, focusing on local issues such as stray and unwanted animals (dogs and cats), draught animals (horses and donkeys), and the illegal wildlife trade. Although they were interested in all animal welfare issues, I felt it was wrong to expect these small groups to use their limited resources and manpower to campaign on other issues for a large international organization, important though as those issues might be.

Importantly, the WSPA also decided to set up an office in China. In my opinion and those of my Chinese contacts, it was not the right time, as the socio-political climate was not stable. At that time in China, the foundations to support animal welfare advocacy were yet to be cemented into the fabric of society. I explained to the new CEO that a WSPA office in China would not be allowed to campaign to ban bear farms from within China. My advice fell on deaf ears.

Now disillusioned with the role I was expected to play and frustrated that although I was Chinese-Taiwanese, my comments were ignored without discussion, in 2004, the following year, I gave up my job after five mostly happy years at the WSPA. Once again plunging into the unknown, I called on fate to guide me to the next stage in my life. By this time, I had met Ross, who was a creative director for BSkyB (now Sky UK). We moved in together and bought a house in a small village some twenty miles outside London, in the leafy suburb of Buckinghamshire. My terraced house in South London was rented out to two of my former WSPA colleagues, so I still had an income. I also did some paid work as a consultant for Care for the Wild International, conducting further research and investigations into the uses of TCM. The organization's CEO, Dr. Barbara Maas, knew of my work with the WSPA as she was also working on animal welfare issues in China and had published the first report on the Chinese fur industry, *Dying for Fur: A Report on the Fur Industry in China*, in collaboration with EAST International and Swiss Animal Protection (SAP).

When I had completed the consultancy, I was again left to ponder my next step. What was I going to do now? In my mind, I went over the events of the past ten years and recalled how in 1996, soon after leaving Taiwan, I had helped organize a humane education training course in France. Humane education is defined as a process that nurtures compassion and respect for people, animals, and the environment and recognizes that all are interrelated and interdependent. Joy and Princess Elisabeth de Croÿ often held training days for the employees at Elisabeth's shelter, Refuge de Thiernay, in central France. Then, they were planning an interactive three-week residential course for twenty selected attendees from Poland, Ukraine, and Taiwan, including veterinarians and students in animal welfare, who needed some practical experience in shelter management and veterinary techniques. The aim of the training sessions was to help them understand the basic concepts of humane education in action.

Most of the attendees had read books and reports on humane education but were unfamiliar with the practical aspects, so there was a big gap in their knowledge and understanding. In addition, the veterinarians, although university-trained, were familiar with treating and handling only large animals, such as cattle and pigs reared for meat. Their veterinary training had not covered companion animals and spay/neuter techniques. Our plan was to help bridge that gap and encourage open discussion, so that they could learn from each other and return to their own countries with new ideas. I remembered that we had invited Dr. Roger Mugford (a renowned international animal behaviorist) to give demonstrations in animal behavior and Dr. David Griffiths (a retired veterinarian who had worked for years in Los Angeles, treating animals belonging to Hollywood film stars) to train our attendees to understand good practice in surgical techniques. It was a memorable and fun-packed learning experience.

Now, in 2004, as I remembered how successful the course in France had been, with all the attendees still working in animal welfare and humane education, I wondered if my next move could be to do something similar. I discussed my tentative ideas with Joy and Janice Cox—a longtime friend, former director at the WSPA, and co-founder of World Animal Net—and we agreed that a sound foundation for humane education and animal welfare was still lacking, as most resource materials prepared by international organizations were pitched at a higher level of understanding while basic information was unavailable in developing countries. We decided to create more suitable resources as our new project, which we called Pioneer Training.

Building on the experience and outcome of the course in France, we decided to create a similar but more intensive residential course and refine some of the activities. We wanted to invite more people than before, so we would need a larger venue, but even after considering many possibilities, we found that a venue for a month-long residential program for some twenty-five people would simply cost too much. Then, by chance, Federico Spinola, a friend of Princess Elisabeth de Croÿ's, gave us a wonderful opportunity. A lifelong supporter of animal welfare, he generously loaned us his palatial home to use for the residential training course. Known as Tenuta Banna Castle, the estate was located in northern Italy, south of Turin, with beautiful gardens including a magical, fairy tale-like wisteria garden. Such a tranquil setting for the inaugural Pioneer Training course!

The invited delegates from eleven countries all responded with enthusiasm to the interactive workshops, specifically designed for a multicultural group, and appreciated the idyllic surroundings. One of the attendees was Vivienne, a South African teacher working in a school in Khayelitsha Township, the largest township in South Africa, thirty kilometers from Cape Town. Established in 1985 under apartheid law, with people with dark skin forcibly and sometimes violently moved there, Khayelitsha Township had evolved into a place of unrest, crime, and violence. Even so, Vivienne was pioneering humane education in her school. She recalled how unique an experience being invited to take part in Pioneer Training with a multicultural group was for her, as she had been brought up during apartheid (1948–1994), when non-white people were not allowed to sit alongside white people. Now, her life had changed beyond anything she could have imagined, and she felt so welcome among like-minded peers at this magnificent venue, sharing knowledge and experiences.

Having worked in large organizations for many years, Janice, Joy, and I shared a similar mindset. As I said previously, there was a big gap in the level of understanding between many of the established international organizations and the small, pioneering groups around the world, with cultural differences being largely ignored. We aimed to bridge that divide by developing workable and realistic strategies to help these pioneers address issues of concern specific to their respective countries.

Following our course, all the delegates returned to their own countries and either set up NGOs or found work within the humane education sector. Their feedback to us, detailing their hopes and plans for the future, was inspirational. One news left us reeling with disbelief, however. Betty Wang, one of the attendees from China, who had been so vocal during the training and so motivated afterwards, tragically died just a few weeks later.

When we returned to the UK after a successful month in Italy, still fired up with enthusiasm, Janice, Joy, and I had a meeting to potentially formalize our emerging plans and establish Pioneer Training as an organization. But for various reasons, we did not reach an agreement, so Pioneer Training was left to rest. As for me, I decided it was an opportune time to start my own organization, which would allow me to take some of the Pioneer Training concepts and tailor them to Asian lifestyles and communities. I began collaborating with two ex-colleagues at the WSPA and shortly after, in May 2006, ACTAsia for Animals was born, with a draft business plan as well as a vision and mission:

> Vision: We believe that respect for people, animals, and the environment will lead to a more compassionate and sustainable world.
> Mission: By educating children, consumers, and professionals, ACTAsia promotes kindness and compassion for people, animals, and the environment among Asian societies.

The (unpaid) founding partners were me as CEO, Deepa Balaram as co-founder, and Nel Amerongen as a part-time fundraiser. We planned to work in China and India simultaneously, as Deepa, being Indian, had contacts there. However, she was unable to leave her paid job for a couple of years, and China became my sole focus.

2007. ACTAsia for Animals' first staff members (volunteers).
Left to right: Pei, Deepa Balaram, Shen Chen, Iso Zhang

My first line of thinking went like this: Most of the people involved in animal welfare advocacy seemed to want to do rescue work, which was desperately needed because there were so many unwanted animals. But facilities dedicated to rescue work seemed to be mainly make-shift sheds or cages, where dogs, cats, donkeys, ducks, chickens, and even wild animals were confined for days, sometimes weeks, months, even years. Perhaps ACTAsia for Animals could build a purpose-made animal sanctuary and use it as a model training center?

I put this suggestion to a few of my friends who were experienced in shelter management. "NO, NO, NO!" they cried. "You don't have the experience or the money. To do it well is a huge job and responsibility. You will need many employees who are experienced and used to handling animals. The ongoing costs are so high, including feeding, maintenance, and veterinary costs. It is so time-consuming that you would become insular and restricted. You are better suited to working internationally as you originally intended." I'm not sure I was convinced, but as I had never worked in a busy animal rescue center for longer than a few days or weeks, I accepted their opinions. (I now know they were right.) But how could I help those who were already doing rescue work and running shelters to aim for higher standards and enhance their understanding of how to ethically manage confined animals? It was obvious: the focus of ACTAsia for Animals would be education and training.

Even now, I often ask myself: "If I could live my life over again, would I start an organization from scratch without even the basic resources?" I suspect I might, as I tend to be stubborn, not always thinking rationally when I get fixated on an idea in my head. But with the benefit of hindsight, it does seem illogical to have gone ahead with such determination. The first five years of ACTAsia were indeed difficult in so many ways: The frustration of having made some solid plans but having no money to act on them. No paid staff. No offices. No organizational profile. Also, an unexpected addition to my family (more about baby Risa in later chapters). Looking back, I can see that it was foolish in the extreme to start a new organization in this way, especially with the aim of working in China—a country with not the best track record in human or animal welfare. So why didn't I focus on Asian countries such as Singapore or Japan, where animal welfare protection and humane education were already in practice? Was there something lying dormant in my subconscious that was steering me toward my father's homeland?

My first fact-finding visit to China as CEO of ACTAsia was made possible by a donation of 1,000 pounds from Princess Elisabeth de Croÿ, who had a particular interest in China and Taiwan. I first met her in 1994 when she came to Taiwan as an international ambassador in support of the LCA's "Disposable Dogs: Made in Taiwan" campaign. She immediately became a great friend to me

2007. ACTAsia 2nd Capacity building course for animal welfare groups in Shenzhen.

and Wu Hung. She had also visited Beijing when she was a young woman and enjoying a high profile as an aristocrat traveling the world. Her life then consisted mainly of flitting from one party to another, enjoying a busy social life in Paris.

But in the 1960s, now in her forties, Elisabeth turned her back on her gilded lifestyle and bought a dilapidated small farm property in rural France using money gifted to her by her aunt. It was a modest amount, but she used it to set up an animal shelter and veterinary clinic for stray and unwanted animals. Spending most of her money on housing for animals, Elisabeth lived in a small cottage at the farm that had not been maintained for many years. There was no heating, electricity, or running water. She registered the premises with the government as a charity, named Défense et Protection des Animaux, with the animal facilities known as Refuge de Thiernay. Today, it is still a leading charity in France.

Her family dating back to the Holy Roman Empire in the twelfth century, Elisabeth was born in a castle and schooled by a governess. She had an upbringing so different from mine. Even so, she saw similarities between the two of us. We both were somewhat rebellious and single-minded, driven and determined to somehow make a difference and forge a pathway to the humane treatment of all living beings. When she gave me the 1,000 pound donation, which she could ill afford, she expressed how much she wished she could come with me to China for my fact-finding mission, but at the time, she was unable to walk without pain, the result of a serious injury to her foot.

I set off for my first ACTAsia mission to China in May 2006, having arranged for Sarah, my school friend from Taiwan, to meet me and do some filming as a record of the meetings that we took part in and the groups that we met. We also went to see my third sister Jessica (Mei Ru), who was now married and living with her husband and daughter in the modern coastal town of Zhuhai, Guangdong Province. She was only too pleased to see me and to hear what I was trying to do. She gave ACTAsia one of its first donations and even offered to become a volunteer.

Before her abrupt death, Betty Wang, whom I had met originally through my work with the WSPA's Asian member societies and again at the Pioneer Training course in Italy, had scheduled me to meet new groups that were either newly formed or during the process of being formed to promote humane education and animal welfare protection. Betty's death tinged my first visit to China with an element of disbelief and intense sadness.

One faces many restrictions when starting a nonprofit in China, where charities like those in Western countries that are registered with the government do not exist. For example, in the UK, the Charity Commission, a government department answerable to Parliament, regulates the work of all registered charities. But in

China, the process is more complex with various options, some being financially expensive. Especially as a nonresident foreigner, I needed to thoroughly research all options before making any quick decisions. At this point, my focus was on making contacts, with one of my first contacts being Iso Zhang, who would prove to be a key figure in the development of ACTAsia China. Dynamic and motivated, Iso was already a pioneer in the development of animal welfare education in Shenzhen. The previous year, she had started Shenzhen Cats, an organization promoting birth control methods to help reduce the number of stray and unwanted cats roaming the streets. The group's volunteers trapped stray cats and had them spayed/neutered at a low cost; once recovered, the cats were put up for adoption on social networking sites. At a later date, Iso and I became the co-founders of ACTAsia China.

The trip to China proved to be useful and confirmed my suspicion that animal welfare protection and humane education were just in their beginnings there. I met many people interested in this work and willing to do it, but collectively, their knowledge of animal sentience and welfare was shallow. Just as I had concluded from Pioneer Training in Italy and from my work with the WSPA's member societies, a basic level of information and knowledge was needed to lay the foundations on which they could then build. I decided that ACTAsia for Animals could best aid in the development of groups by focusing on the capacity-building model for the first few years.

With this at the forefront of my mind, I worked toward organizing a series of workshops and training sessions in three major cities: through open discussions, participants explored the interrelationship between people and animals and learned of recent scientific studies on animal sentience, behavior, and welfare. But although I was convinced that I was on the right track, I knew that this work was not attractive to potential donors. All of the newspaper reports and anecdotal comments I was able to gather about cruelties committed against people and animals in China helped me understand that ACTAsia for Animals needed to do some thorough countrywide research.

With China being one of the largest countries on Earth, with a population of 1.3 billion people (in 2006) living in thirty-four provinces and administrative areas, it was obvious to me that there would be significant differences in the lifestyles and attitudes of people living in different areas, especially autonomous ones. In the previous twenty years, China had enjoyed a period of growing prosperity, which delighted some people but left others feeling fearful as their rural lifestyles were disappearing and their villages being destroyed. A government policy encouraged people to move from rural areas to the cities, where work was plentiful thanks to a booming construction industry and rapid economic growth. However, this meant that children and the elderly were often left behind, confused and disoriented, in deserted and dying villages.

With the help of contacts I made in Shenzhen, Changsha, and Beijing during my visit, during the next few months, we conducted countrywide research and collated the information in book format, which we published under the title *Changing China*. The book, which detailed the social implications of the Chinese political system, was subsequently used as a bible of sorts by international organizations working on humanitarian issues in China. It was essential that any international organization that wanted to approach the government understood the socio-political context. As there was so much interest in *Changing China*, I contacted many international organizations and individuals to ask if they would be able to support our work there. Despite the general interest in China, a country still swathed in mystery, I received only a couple of tentative offers of help. I now had to decide whether I could find the funding to build and maintain an organization or this was just a fantasy I had built up in my mind.

It was now 2007: ACTAsia for Animals was officially registered with the Charity Commission in the UK as a nonprofit company, thanks to a generous sponsor who had covered all costs for the registration process. I knew there was much to be done in China in terms of education and training, so I decided I would press on. I now knew of many amazing and inspiring people, one of them being the remarkable Jane Goodall, who had defied all odds to pursue studying primates in Africa. Having read many books on her life and work, I could identify with her love for animals and the natural world. Without conventional qualifications, she nevertheless took initiative and persevered until others in her field had to acknowledge that she was indeed capable and doing valuable work. Gradually, she gained credibility and became the foremost expert on chimpanzees. Dr. Goodall made a groundbreaking discovery in 1960 while studying social and family interactions among wild chimpanzees in Gombe Stream National Park in Tanzania, observing that the chimpanzees made and used tools in addition to displaying other human-like behaviors. In her career, she also created a youth education program known as Roots and Shoots, now in sixty-five countries. I was inspired by this woman who created her own path in life based on a mission she believed in. I was determined to do likewise.

Without a salary, I now needed some other way to make money to afford my personal living expenses and enable ACTAsia for Animals to make headway in China. I decided to sell my house in South London and live on the profit while I established the organization and found streams of income for its work. My luck was in: house prices were rapidly rising in London and the once-unfashionable southern areas of London were starting to become desirable. My house sold quickly at a very good price; for once in my life and to my great delight, I now had a cushion in the bank that would enable me to realize the dreams I had been playing out in my mind day and night for a long time. As it turned out, I had sold my house at just the right time: shortly after, the housing market crashed and the global financial crisis took hold.

2014. Pei meeting children at one of the first CFL Pilot Project schools.

I also continued to receive a few small donations from kind supporters; the money went toward workshops in China covering topics such as legislation, human and animal welfare, environmental concerns, animal handling, animal sentience and behavior. Iso Zhang coordinated the practical and logistical matters, and I designed the course content. On occasion, if funds allowed, I would take a volunteer international expert with me to add greater expertise and credibility to the trainings.

In 2008, I found a supportive and understanding friend in John Ruane, CEO of Naturewatch Foundation. Having set up the organization in 1995, he knew how financially difficult the first few years could be. He generously offered to donate 35,000 pounds a year to ACTAsia for Animals for the first two years, as well as to promote our education and training work on his website. This was an act of tremendous faith and support from a small charity. I asked John, "How long does it take to establish a new organization and find regular streams of income?" He replied, "Ten to fifteen years." So, by John's reckoning, I still had many years to go. At the time, I laughed with him while thinking to myself, *I can do it in a much shorter time than that.* In the end, his words proved to be right.

Sadly, John died in 2013 at the age of sixty-one, but his legacy lives on through the excellent work of Naturewatch Foundation.

2013. Arts & Culture FurFree Outreach Festival in Shenzhen.

Chapter 12

Tenth Anniversary Celebrations

In this chapter, I will try to explain how ACTAsia's vision and mission have evolved by giving an overview of the work I lead and why I do it. It offers not a full picture but a snapshot of the organization's main activities. Although I am the CEO, it's a hands-on role and I am fully involved in the day-to-day management and the practicalities of ACTAsia. During the first five years, I flew to China twice each year to observe firsthand how civic society functioned and to visit fledgling groups there to see how we might assist them further, especially as China was changing and now starting to welcome foreign enterprise, although the government still retained ultimate control.

Despite my being half Chinese, I grew up and spent a significant portion of my adulthood in Taiwan, and my experiences were informed by a different socio-political environment compared to those born and raised in China. Taiwan has, in the past forty years, transitioned peacefully from authoritarianism to a well-functioning democracy, whereas China's government is described in the very Constitution of the People's Republic of China as a "people's democratic dictatorship." Although Taiwan views itself as an independent country, with its own constitution and democratically elected leaders, the Chinese government insists that Taiwan is a breakaway province of China, one that will eventually be under Beijing's control again.

A few years after I co-founded ACTAsia for Animals, Iso Zhang was now our representative in China and she registered the organization with the authorities as a social enterprise. All of my meetings with Iso as well as with animal welfare groups, local public health officials, and veterinarians helped me build up a picture of the main issues and our priorities in China. From individual anecdotes and public records of human and animal abuse, I identified an apparent lack of compassion and empathy in Chinese society toward humans, animals, and the environment. In addition, there was no effective legal framework to hold offenders responsible for their abusive behavior, so it was rare for any action to be taken against them.

I decided that the best use of our resources would be to introduce humane education—an education that recognized people, animals, and the environment as interrelated and interdependent—into primary schools. I recalled the humane education workshops I had been a part of in France and in Italy—how successful they proved to be over time and how many of the attendees were now either leading their own organizations or working with international organizations in the field.

Iso and I agreed that to give humane education the best chance of survival in China, we needed to launch our program in a province known to be progressive, then promote that first iteration as a model for other provinces to copy. Fortunately, Iso and my third sister Jessica lived in two major cities in Guangdong—Iso in Shenzhen and Jessica in Zhuhai—both ideal locations to launch an education program in primary schools. Iso, who had been working with me for the last five years, offered to approach the education authorities in Shenzhen, while Jessica would reach out to schools in Zhuhai, where she was on the committee of the parent–teacher association at her daughter's primary school.

Tenacious and well-organized, both Jessica and Iso were able to give professional and persuasive presentations to the schools, introducing ACTAsia for Animals' approach to compassionate education. Five schools were willing to be in the pilot project, agreeing to incorporate this new way of teaching at the beginning of the next academic school year as it was complementary to the mandatory curriculum subject Moral Education.

At this stage, I just had the idea of humane education lessons in mind; I hadn't given much thought to the implementation process, though I felt that it was a good idea in concept, one that could work. Having no suitable resource materials for the classroom, I contacted large organizations in many countries such as the US, UK, and Australia to ask if we could use their humane education materials and lesson plans, which were comprehensive, attractive in design and content, and which the organizations were willing to share. We realized, however, that we needed lesson plans with much simpler, more basic messages for Chinese schools. As our research had highlighted, many children and parents considered toy animals and real animals to be in much the same category and equally dispensable. Also, with most schoolchildren being only children due to the government's One Child Policy, introduced in 1979, children lacked an understanding of basic social skills such as sharing with and caring for each other.

Thus, relying mainly on ideas from other organizations and free lesson plans from the internet, ACTAsia for Animals' UK staff and a volunteer teacher in China created simplified, translated lessons and classroom activities for a twelve-month pilot project. To our delight, the schools were enthusiastic and asked for similar lessons for older children, so we got to creating more lessons and activities for the following school year.

We named the program Caring for Life (CFL) Education, and word spread quickly as we now had contacts in other areas, leading to more schools wanting to join the project. I decided this program was too good for us to stop here, instead it should become a six-year curriculum to cover all primary/elementary schooling. None of us in the organization at that time had the expertise to write an academic curriculum; moreover, we were working on a shoestring budget. We needed to find someone to do this work at a reasonable cost. In hindsight, it was a miracle that we had even come this far, mainly thanks to the generosity of Iso, who used her own money to keep ACTAsia for Animals afloat, and the expertise of Jessica, who controlled the budget and had a rare magic touch that made one dollar do the work of ten dollars.

Then, by chance, a contact of ours in Singapore suggested a local businessman might be willing to sponsor the CFL education project. Nervously, I approached our potential sponsor and held my breath, not daring to hope for success. To my delight, he agreed to support most of the project for three years. We were on our way! We just needed to find the rest of the necessary funding. Contacts from experienced organizations warned us that it was difficult to raise funds for education projects, with donors preferring rescue work. But now, with at least some money, we set out to find someone who would design a professional curriculum at a low cost.

Fortunately, Nick Leney, whom I had known since my first arrival in the UK, was an experienced international curriculum designer and agreed to work with us. Together, we produced what is now a multi-award-winning curriculum of CFL education for schools. I asked Nick to design a curriculum that would cover all six years of primary/elementary schooling, made up of five subject areas—Web of Life, Sentience, Care and Respect, Interacting with Others, and Emotional Intelligence—and sixty lessons to be taught during two academic terms of each school year.

Nick based the curriculum on the United Nations' Four Pillars of Education, focusing on the pillar Learning to Live Together to encourage a holistic view of the relationships between humans, animals, and the environment and promote lifelong learning. He visualized the CFL education model, with its five subject areas, as an integrated, progressive spiral, with three interlocking themes: Know the World, Sense the World, and Participate in the World. All of our lessons were created based on inquiry learning with age-appropriate activities, a method that helped children learn through being involved and encouraged critical thinking.

My vision was that CFL education in schools would teach children to become more compassionate and empathetic. The six-year curriculum would help each child develop their emotional intelligence, thus shaping their character so that they would grow into a respectful and responsible global citizen.

Once we had the curriculum and lesson materials translated into the Chinese language, we had to teach the teachers how to use them. In China, teachers were trained to use the rote method, meaning there was little interaction or two-way communication between teacher and child. It was a big challenge for the teachers to learn new methods. Some were keen and willing to cooperate, but others did not want the extra work and gave up. Nevertheless, generally, the children loved to take part in the activities and to voice their opinions. The CFL project was now becoming noticed in China. In 2015, we would receive our first two national awards.

CFL in English

CFL in Chinese

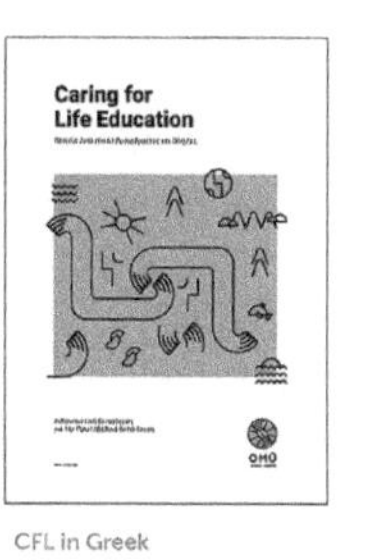

CFL in Greek

CFL in Sindhi

2022. Caring for Life education lesson plans in four languages: English, Chinese, Greek & Sindhi.

The same year, I was asked to present on CFL education at a conference in the US. At the end of the conference, I spoke to Dr. William Samuels, Director of Accreditation and Assessment at the City University of New York, who was particularly interested in research on the impact of humane education as few studies had been done anywhere in the world, none using large samples and spanning a long period of time. I asked if he would be interested in helping us evaluate our program in the schools in China where CFL education was being pioneered, as I had wanted an independent evaluation right from the start. He immediately agreed and generously offered his time and expertise.

Bill's first visit to China was with me in 2013; now, ten years later, he continues to work with us, conducting further studies on our CFL program. Back in my WSPA days, I had already started thinking about how humane education lessons could be evaluated: without scientific evaluation, any such program, however good it might be, would lack credibility and therefore not be easily accepted by education authorities as an important addition to schools' curricula. Bill spent hours patiently discussing with me and explaining how we might be able to do the research in China, especially given the importance of accurate data collection and interpretation. His first studies for ACTAsia for Animals evaluated the pro-social behaviors of children before and after CFL lessons.

Bill's work has helped to build credibility for my organization. He has now conducted several studies for us; he has presented the results at international conferences and published them in scientific journals. He is currently working on an evaluation of the effects of CFL education on the behaviors of autistic children.

My visit to the US proved to be helpful to ACTAsia for Animals in more ways than one, as I also met Ken Swensen, who eventually became our volunteer fundraiser in the US and played a key role in developing our first business plan. His tenacious fundraising has enabled us to expand the CFL Education program to other schools in China and also to develop the CFL Fur-Free Fashion project.

One day, one of our volunteers in China, Justine Wong, asked if her new farm park might be helpful for CFL practical lessons, in which children would be taught how to safely interact with animals. My response was an enthusiastic "Yes, please." In the park, children could learn how to handle animals and would see them amidst natural surroundings, with the wooded areas also providing opportunities for lessons about trees, flowers, and the small creatures living among the vegetation. Justine kept all species of animals at her farm, large (horses, pigs, goats) and small (rabbits, dogs, cats), so for children who had never experienced close contact with animals in their everyday lives, these outdoor learning opportunities added an interesting and complementary dimension to the theory learned in the classroom.

Now, ten years later, CFL education continues to be a great success in schools in China, and we have incorporated into our lessons the United Nations' Sustainable Development Goals (SDGs), a set of common goals designed to bring people together to improve lives around the world. The SDGs address global challenges such as poverty, inequality, and climate change, while aiming to harmonize three core components—economic growth, social inclusion, and environmental protection.

To date, CFL education has reached more than 300,000 children in 600 schools and education centers, with almost 4,000 teachers trained by ACTAsia. In 2021, some of our lessons were adapted by Dawn Kotuwage, an experienced teacher who joined ACTAsia in 2019 as International Projects Director. Previously, Dawn had been a senior lecturer in an agricultural college. She had also lived and worked in the animal welfare movement in several Asian countries—Thailand, Malaysia, Indonesia, Sri Lanka, and India—resulting in a rich repertoire of firsthand knowledge of several Asian cultures and lifestyles. The adapted lessons reflect changes in learning theory in recent years and include greater emphasis on prominent current issues such as climate change and the environmental implications of the intensive farming industry.

So far in this chapter, I have attempted to give just a very brief overview of ACTAsia's work in schools and how it began. Reading through this summary, you may get the impression that our journey has always been logical and easy. This could not be further from reality. Our work has been extremely labor-intensive. The huge investment in time and human resources to keep projects alive and functioning cannot be easily measured. Translation of materials was always tricky and complex: the original lessons were written in English, translated into Chinese, and then translated back into English to make sure the concepts were accurately written in Chinese. There were many discrepancies and misinterpretations that we had to correct. And since some English words and Western concepts have no equivalents in the Chinese language, we had to invent alternative terminology.

Other challenges came from the lack of sustained interest from some of the teachers, from the need for repeated explanations of simple concepts such as inquiry learning and endless attempts to convince teachers that critical thinking does not imply negative criticism. Equally frustrating was having to repeatedly explain to teachers, our staff, the media—in fact, to anyone who would listen—the meaning of animal sentience and of compassion in action. I've found myself becoming exasperated on numerous occasions, despite my trying to take a step back and remember that political environment has significant long-term effects on individual thinking and behavior—that in China, people tend to be told what rather than how to think.

Furthermore, traveling to different areas to recruit schools was time-consuming and expensive. During the setting up of our CFL research project and subsequent data collection, we sometimes ran into teachers who were reluctant to do more than their work contracts required. Low staff retention, since we paid rather low wages, led to problems, disruptions, and inefficiencies as we had to continuously recruit and train new staff and volunteers. But despite the numerous setbacks, we survived and forged a path onward. In addition to our work in schools, Iso Zhang also pushed outreach CFL lessons at summer camps for youngsters known as "left-behind children." In China's remote rural areas, there were more than seventy millions of these children, who lived in poverty where endemic diseases were rife and no medical attention was available. Their parents having left for large cities thousands of miles away to look for work, mainly in the government-funded construction industry, these children were abandoned at home with an elderly relative or a family friend, sometimes even on their own. Unable to afford the costs, parents often returned home only once a year and rarely saw their children. (The government has now made a commitment to lift left-behind children out of poverty by the year 2025 and has begun working on that goal.)

Many years later, as I write this book, I can see clearly the impact CFL education is having. One of the most powerful testimonials we have

2018. Kiki, ACTAsia's Youth Ambassador presenting CFL education to her classmates.

was written by Kiki, ACTAsia's Youth Ambassador and the daughter of one of our volunteers. Having completed six years of CFL education, Kiki is now a University student, an influencer and changemaker. A presentation she has broadcast shows just how progressive her mindset is and how she is influencing her peers to consider the ethics of their eating habits and move toward more compassionate lifestyles.

An excerpt from Kiki's presentation:

> When I was young, I overheard what my mom and her colleagues said in a discussion about Caring for Life education and it had a big impact on me. As I grew older and studied CFL at school and learned about the world, I needed to do something about animals and environmental protection.
>
> It's not that people are selfish or don't have empathy, but they don't know the truth—they don't know how much damage their actions bring to our planet. That's why it's even more important for people who do know to take responsibility and spread compassion and empathy—not only for animals, but compassion and empathy also play a vital role in human relationships. When people care for each other and understand each other, there will be less conflict in society.
>
> If people become the best they can be and cherish natural resources, we can create a greener Earth together. Cultivating a sense of compassion and empathy in children will make this process much less tortuous, as they will form our new civic society. I believe that such programs in schools are an indispensable part of our youth's growth, just like Math and English.
>
> During the past year, I was motivated to write a speech about sustainability because every day at school, I saw my friends' buying drinks in plastic bottles and I thought, *How incredible that just one class can create so much garbage!* The experts have told us the importance of protecting the environment, so why can't we do it? I believe many students will have grown up after the COVID-19 pandemic and [taken to heart] the lessons it has taught us.
>
> Every life deserves to be respected, whether it's the person who harms others or the animal [who] is harmed; all deserve to be loved. I think that is my deepest experience.

People have often asked me: "China is a huge country. Do you really expect to reach every school in China?" And every time, I have replied: "Yes. Perhaps not in my lifetime, but I believe it is possible. Kiki has shown how this can be done, and potentially there is a Kiki in every school." Humane education works when we sow the seeds of compassion by touching a few people with the truth, who in turn touch others, so that the message is spread at exponential speed.

As I continued working with schools in China while learning about the work culture and social issues of concern here, I decided I did not want ACTAsia for Animals to be known as just an animal protection organization; it was becoming so much more. I made a conscious decision to restructure our work to address in equal measure issues affecting humans, animals, and the environment. While the CFL curriculum was designed to reflect this holistic view, given our limited income and human resources, we had concentrated mainly on animal welfare and well-being. Now, the time was right for us to align our work with the holistic approach as we had always intended. Iso had already started doing this by collaborating with Suzhou University of Science and Technology (approx. 50 miles from Shanghai), where CFL education has now become a compulsory module for a degree course because compared to traditional models, a holistic approach better serves the learning needs of students who are training to become teachers.

So, I re-registered the charity ACTAsia for Animals as simply ACTAsia, and Caring for Life Education became the umbrella name for ACTAsia's three main projects: Education for Children, Education for Professionals (mainly veterinarians, teachers, and social workers), and Education/Public Awareness for Consumers. Throughout all areas of learning, we maintain a strong theme of compassion in order to promote positive action informed by kindness and understanding.

It was now 2016. CFL education was starting to become known in several provinces in China, and all of ACTAsia's limited resources were focused on expanding the CFL network. But in the UK, few people had heard of ACTAsia, and we were still dependent on mainly volunteers. To raise the profile of ACTAsia, we decided to have a public relations event to celebrate the organization's tenth anniversary later that year.

We knew that for high-profile public relations events, leading charities often organized receptions at the Palace of Westminster in London. I discussed with my colleagues the possibility of holding a reception to introduce the work of ACTAsia in China and CFL education to a new audience, hoping this would help sway potential funders. But would it be too ambitious for a small, unknown charity to try to follow the lead of larger charities? Would it be too expensive to hire one of the stately rooms for an event? The thought of it was exciting, but could we really make it happen?

2016. Pei celebrating ACTAsia's Tenth Anniversary at the China office.

The Palace of Westminster, which was built in 1016, is arguably the most majestic building in the UK; informally known as the Houses of Parliament, it is home to the House of Commons and the House of Lords, the two houses of the UK Parliament. At the north end of the building stands the world-famous clock tower that houses the great bell of the Big Ben, which can be heard on TV and the radio every day, striking the hours. If we wanted to attract prominent members of the public and raise the profile of ACTAsia, there was no better place in the country to stage an event.

My old-time friend Brian, now Chairman of ACTAsia's Board of Trustees, came to our aid. Through his local political activities, he knew Helen Hayes, his Member of Parliament, so he asked her if she would act as guarantor for ACTAsia and give the opening speech at our evening reception. In addition, Baroness Tessa Jowell, former government Cabinet Minister, also agreed to take part. To have the support of such high-profile people was a fantastic start for us.

Our plans became more ambitious, and I managed to persuade a young entrepreneur in the beauty/fashion industry from China to not only financially sponsor the event but also attend with a team of his employees as guests of honor. He was delighted and flattered to be asked to speak at such a prestigious location. And so the event on the tenth day of the tenth month to celebrate ACTAsia's tenth anniversary became a reality, with approximately 100 guests in attendance. Although in such a formal setting, it was a warm and relaxed gathering. The two Members of Parliament, the organization's Chairman, the sponsor of the reception, and I gave brief presentations and information boards on the work of ACTAsia, leaving plenty of time for informal discussions among attendees. The evening was a great success and source of motivation for me, my staff, and volunteers. I vowed that in another ten years, ACTAsia would be a leading force in Asia.

2016. The group from China visiting the University of Oxford Radcliffe Observatory.

In the days following the event, I led the event sponsor and the other members of the group from China on a brief tour of other parts of the UK. One of ACTAsia's trustees, Dr. Helen Winter, who was completing her PhD at the University of Oxford's Green Templeton College, arranged for us to tour the school's premises, a three-acre property where stood the beautiful eighteenth-century Radcliffe Astronomical Observatory. Used as a working observatory from 1773 to 1934, it now formed part of the college's general facilities. We were especially fortunate as the observatory was not open to the public and could only be accessed by special arrangement.

It was during this visit that I was introduced to Emeritus Professor Terence Ryan, a retired doctor and academic, now a joint curator with Professor David Cranston at the Osler-McGovern Centre Museum. The museum, now part of Green Templeton College, was the home of Sir William Osler, an eminent and influential physician, who was touted as a father of modern medicine. Canadian by birth, Osler was one of the founders of John Hopkins Hospital in the US, then later moved to the University of Oxford as Regius Professor of Medicine, a prestigious position originally created by King Henry VIII in 1546. Osler remained working at Oxford until his death in 1919. His unique, kindly bedside manner, prioritizing the well-being of each of his patients in their recovery, gave an added dimension to his medical practice.

During my discussions with Professor Ryan, I found that the philosophy of William Osler rang true in my mind, in particular his widely quoted saying: "The practice of medicine is an art, not a trade; a calling, not a business; a calling in which your heart will be

2018. WSAVA/ACTAsia Veterinary Training Conference, celebrating ten years of training in China.

exercised equally with your head." As I learned more about Osler's humanitarian as opposed to strictly scientific approach to his work, I could clearly see a strong common thread between his work and ACTAsia's. For Osler, the well-being of each patient was of utmost importance in the decision-making process. Likewise, the well-being of each individual animal was a concept I was trying to instill into the veterinarians attending our training courses in China. Also, Osler's words, as quoted by Professor David Cranston in his book *William Osler and His Legacy to Medicine*, could be equally applied to the veterinary profession: "As doctors we are not only clinicians and teachers, but we are also role models for those around us. When we teach at the bedside or in clinic, we are watched and observed as to how we treat our patients and our staff. It gives insight into our values in life, our goals and beliefs."

A working relationship developed between ACTAsia and the Osler-McGovern Centre. In 2019, the centenary year of Osler's death, Professor Ryan organized a series of five seminars there to celebrate Osler's life and lasting influence. ACTAsia was invited to collaborate on the first seminar, titled "Health and Well-Being: Science and Humanity Are One; Care Technology Applied with Care Attitude." At this event, we launched iCARE, an ACTAsia initiative for CFL education and research in collaboration with international universities. iCARE aims to address evolving life challenges by progressing a holistic One Health approach, recognizing the interrelationship between humans, animals, and the environment.

Professor Ryan, a nonagenarian, is an inspiration and role model for me. His enthusiasm for life and for promoting kindness, friendship, and patience has inspired me to follow his lead, being ever mindful of my own attitudes and behavior. He is now a trustee of the ACTAsia UK Board, continuing to offer us his invaluable wisdom and support.

2018. ACTAsia Train the Trainer veterinarians. Left to right: Dr. Rebecca Wright (New Zealand VFC), Dr. Elaine Ong (Australia, VFC Founder), Dr. Jason Yeh (Taiwan)

Chapter 13

New Horizons

I have long been aware that veterinarians have an important role to play in society, not only as healthcare professionals but also as teachers, especially as there is a strong correlation between the abuse of animals and that of humans, including domestic abuse and child abuse. As summed up by a publication of the American Humane Association, *Understanding the Link between Violence to People and Violence to Animals*: "When animals are abused, people are at risk; when people are abused, animals are at risk."

I have mentioned in earlier chapters that in China, the concept of animal welfare is still poorly understood; even the well-being of dogs and cats—of companion animals in general—tends to be of little concern to guardians. Sadly, this also applies to some veterinarians, especially those in remote rural areas. Keeping pets is a relatively new practice in China, with many guardians seeing their pets as novelty items and not giving too much thought to their responsibility to the animals. When the animals are not their own, some even take extreme actions such as using poisoned bait, wanting to get rid of the noise or fearing transmissible diseases.

Veterinarians in China do not have the same professional status as their counterparts do in most of the Western world; here, promoting animal welfare is not an usual part of the vocation, as veterinarians' university training focuses on treating animals in the food industry, with no tuition relating to companion animals. While

2020. Qinghai shepherd bringing puppy for vaccination, worming, and neutering to the ACTAsia veterinary training clinic.

Chinese people have not traditionally kept pets, in recent years, rapid economic growth and the resulting affluence have created an increasing demand for pedigree puppies and kittens, seen as luxury items. Other animals such as rabbits have also become popular pets. As guardians have little understanding of the needs of these animals and no one to turn to for advice, veterinarians need to quickly develop the knowledge and skills to meet the demand.

In one instance, a lady at one of ACTAsia's workshops explained that she loved having a rabbit as a pet but found it distressing that each one she had kept became ill and died of some mystery illness that her veterinarian couldn't identify. When we asked her some basic questions such as what foods the rabbits ate, the mystery of their short lives was easily solved. Thinking they were being very kind, the lady and her husband fed their rabbits a meat diet, the same diet they themselves enjoyed, not realizing that evolution equipped rabbits with a digestive system that needs fiber, exactly what meat lacks. Unable to digest the fiber-deficient and fat- and protein-heavy meat, the rabbits died from malnutrition. To someone from a Western country, it would seem almost unbelievable that someone could make this mistake, as many children get a rabbit as their first pet and quickly learn what types of food rabbits eat. There are simply worded books about the habits and behaviors of different animal species so that children can readily learn how to take care of their pets, and there are numerous free leaflets on display in pet shops and veterinarians' waiting rooms for the parents of those children.

I decided that ACTAsia could bring in international veterinarians to train local vets in China, who would then be able to train their colleagues, in line with a tried and tested model known as Train the Trainer. We set up the scheme for regular training workshops held in cooperation with municipality veterinarians, using local government veterinary premises, and led by Dr. Chris Barton and Dr. Elaine Ong, founders of Vets for Compassion Australia (VFC). Now, although both Chris and Elaine run busy veterinary clinics in Melbourne, they still find the time to train veterinarians in Asian countries; twice each year, they bring their own veterinary nurses to China to train technicians, with all the expenses raised through VFC. Chris and Elaine have also written a comprehensive veterinary training guide specific to the needs and resources of Chinese veterinarians, which was published by ACTAsia and continues to be used in trainings.

By the end of 2019, CFL education was well established in China, and ACTAsia's projects educating children, veterinarians, and consumers had earned us fifteen awards in seven years. CFL education had also been introduced to schools in Pakistan and Greece. I was regularly invited to speak at international conferences and sit on expert panels. The Train the Trainer model had been a key feature of CFL education for veterinarians for thirteen years. Also in 2019, the World Small Animal Veterinary Association (WSAVA) selected ACTAsia to

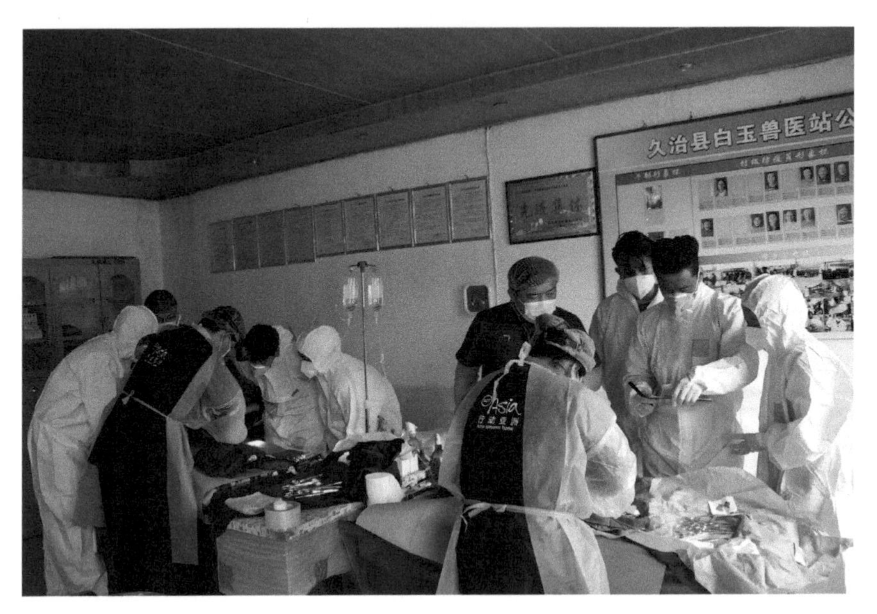

2017. ACTAsia veterinary training clinic in Qinghai.

be its education partner in Asia. This was a wonderful endorsement for ACTAsia and brought us widespread recognition, as the WSAVA is a well-established organization with more than 200,000 veterinarians in 110 member associations from eighty-seven countries.

One of the veterinary training sessions took us to Qinghai, a remote inland rural province in central-west China, adjacent to the Tibet Autonomous Region in the southwest and the Uygur Autonomous Region of Xinjiang in the northwest. In this part of China, most of the inhabited land is situated at high altitudes, up to 3,500 meters above sea level, surrounded by mountains and plateaus. Qinghai is the largest province in China by area yet the most sparsely populated, with just over 5 million people of thirty-seven ethnic nationalities.

I was excited to be setting up a project in Qinghai, especially as I was liaising with a conservation group that was working to protect wildlife in the national parks there. Traditionally, the population in the area had practiced nomadic farming, but in recent years, the government had developed a policy to prevent nomads from moving from place to place, so they had to give up their preferred lifestyle and settle in one area. No longer on the move, they also no longer needed to keep dogs to guard livestock save for one or two, so surplus dogs were left to roam. This led to an increase in stray dogs fighting for food and attacking other species, domesticated and wild. But even more problematic was echinococcus, a zoonotic parasitic disease spread by the roaming dogs.

Echinococcus is a serious, life-threatening disease caused by a particular class of parasitic tapeworms; it can pass from a host to humans and other animals, mainly sheep, cows, goats, camels, and yaks, through tapeworm eggs contained in food, water, or soil or through direct contact. The parasite can cause large cysts to develop in the lungs and liver, affecting organ function and resulting in death. The municipality was keen for international veterinarians to come to Qinghai and teach local veterinarians how to control the dog population with spay/neuter techniques and how to prevent echinococcus with regular deworming, per the WHO's recommendations.

As local veterinarians were trained primarily to treat primarily farmed animals, not small animals, they lacked clinical experience and practical knowledge of how to handle dogs and tended to be wary of the larger dogs in the area. These were heavy-boned, Tibetan Mastiff-type dogs with dense double coats to protect them from the harsh weather. Their ancestors came from the harsh Himalayan mountains, so the breed had evolved to withstand the most hostile climate conditions. Traditionally used as livestock guardian dogs, with a reputation as the most ferocious of the guardian breeds, they were fearless and known to defend the herd against flying predators, coyotes, and even bears.

Once the veterinary training course had been arranged, our whole team was scheduled to meet in Xining, the capital city of Qinghai

Province. I traveled to Qinghai from Shanghai (a journey of around eight hours), others from different cities in China, and the international team from VFC all the way from Melbourne, Australia. We had arranged to stay overnight in Xining, located at 2,275 meters, to try to adjust to the altitude before climbing higher. It usually takes a few days to get used to a high altitude as the air pressure is lower and there is less oxygen, making it difficult to breathe, but as seasoned travelers, we thought twenty-four hours should be sufficient for us to acclimate.

Our team included eight veterinarians from different parts of China (all trained by ACTAsia and now certified as Master Trainers), the international team from VFC Australia, and ACTAsia personnel tasked with filming and documenting the project. In Xining, I held a briefing with the whole team to explain the aims and objectives of the project, as well as the local context. The equipment was checked, with the surgical kits and consumable materials having been sourced mainly from other cities in China; such equipment was either limited or not available in Qinghai Province.

The next day, it was time to set off for our destination, Baiyu, approximately 1,500 kilometers away. We traveled in four eight-seater cars, with one vehicle transporting the equipment and other resources. During the fifteen-hour journey, we had to make unplanned stops as many on the team became victims of the high altitude and started vomiting. As for me, I realized, a little too late, that I had made a big mistake in not preparing enough warm clothes and not wearing the right type of shoes.

Before traveling, I had checked the average temperature for Qinghai at that time of year; the report said around fifteen degrees, which seemed agreeable. What I didn't know was that although it was around fifteen degrees during the day, the temperature dropped to five degrees at night and in the early morning, and the atmosphere was very damp. I was shivering even though I had several layers

2020. Group photo in Qinghai. The monks encouraged the public to have their dogs neutered and wormed against echinococcus at the ACTAsia vet training sessions.

on, and since my shoes were not waterproof, my feet felt damp and icy cold. I started to develop a throbbing headache, with feelings of dizziness and confusion, not unlike jet lag symptoms. Then, when I started vomiting, feeling weak and exhausted, memories of altitude sickness came flooding back as I recalled my hiking days in Taiwan.

We were staying at a bed-and-breakfast, the newest building in town albeit very basic, three stories high, the guest rooms being on the third floor. There was just one bathroom that was shared between ten rooms and positioned about thirty meters from my room. The toilet was not connected to a water supply, so after using it, we had to scoop water out of a large, deep bucket in the bathroom to flush, all this without any light. After repeating this flushing ritual in the dark for twelve hours straight as I was vomiting and simultaneously suffering from diarrhea, I became paranoid that I might drown in the water bucket. I felt incredibly weak, and the lack of cleanliness at our accommodation was concerning.

Although I knew I was dehydrated, I was too scared to go to the local hospital, being skeptical of the medical standards and general hygiene there. So, knowing that I could not be persuaded to go, the veterinarians inserted an intravenous drip into my arm and took turns to watch over me for the rest of the night. I told one of the Master Trainer veterinarians that as I had trained him and his colleagues for the past ten years, I trusted them to keep me alive. How ironic that their first patient in Qinghai was me, a human animal!

The next day, I had to get up for an interview for the film we were making about why we were in Qinghai and what we were doing. By this time, I was feeling much better compared to the day before and managed to get through the filming without any difficulties. It's incredible to think that only a few hours earlier, I had been crawling along the corridor from my room to the bathroom at the bed-and-breakfast—the human body and mind can be so resilient.

Notwithstanding the hiccups caused by our bouts of altitude sickness, the training program continued as planned and attracted more than thirty public veterinarians, along with government officials, from six provinces.

We entered into a three-year agreement with the Qinghai government to deliver more training sessions, but the COVID-19 pandemic prevented us from returning in 2020 and 2021. We then planned to restart in late 2022, but unfortunately, our plans had to be changed yet again. The training schedule has now been rearranged eight times; at the time of writing, COVID-19 is still active in China and the government is upholding its zero COVID policy. Although frustrating, situations like this are not unusual given that we work internationally and many factors are out of our control, including sudden changes in the local environment, the weather, and personnel. We eventually returned in 2023.

2015. International Cruelty-Free Fashion Show in Beijing.

Accompanying Caring for Life education for schoolchildren and professionals is the third strand of ACTAsia's work, Caring for Life education for consumers, which focuses on compassionate lifestyle choices. This is probably the hardest area in which to effect change, but now, through social media, we can reach millions of people in China with our message, and one of the things we promote is compassion in fashion. Through annual fashion shows and forums showcasing sustainable fashion garments, supported by leading fashion houses, we create awareness of the suffering involved in the animal fur and animal skin trades as well as of the potential dangers to human health of the carcinogenic chemicals used in processing systems.

Traditionally, people in China wore fur as protection from the extreme cold characteristic of the northeastern region, but since the middle of the twentieth century, fur has also become a fashion item. The fur industry has flourished alongside economic growth, owing to the popularity of and increasing demand for fur items. China is the biggest importer of fur pelts globally and the biggest user of fur garments, with the supply coming from wild animals such as mink, foxes, chinchillas, rabbits, and raccoon dogs, either farmed for their furs or trapped in the wild, and even stolen cats and dogs.

Aside from animal welfare concerns, the human health implications of the fur industry are of great concern to ACTAsia, and we have conducted research into the potential dangers of the toxic chemicals found in fur clothing. After an animal is killed, his pelt (his skin with the hair still attached) is sent away to be tanned, dyed, or bleached using chemicals known to be carcinogenic and toxic to humans. These chemicals can find their way into the human bloodstream from just a small fur trim or a fur keychain. Many garments for babies and children have fur trims, but since product labeling is not stringently controlled by Chinese law, buyers in China and in other countries are not aware of the dangers. In addition, workers in the fur industry are offered no protection from the carcinogens or the other harmful chemicals they are in contact with on a regular basis. And last but not least, the industry's environmental neglect in routinely dumping toxic waste into rivers and lakes puts the public at great risk.

ACTAsia has been working with the London College of Fashion (LCF) for the past five years, and during three of those five years, Dawn Kotuwage has worked in collaboration with the Dean of Academic Strategy, John Lau, to produce a Sustainable Fashion curriculum for a fur-free future. The curriculum is currently being used at universities in China, and Dawn is also giving online tuition to students in other countries, emphasizing the need for compassion in the fashion industry. The course is divided into three modules on the importance of environmental preservation for a better future; the need to protect the natural, raw materials that we are consuming at an unsustainable rate; and the waste produced by the fashion industry and means of reducing it.

We do not want ACTAsia to be known as a judgmental, dictatorial type of organization that condemns the fur industry and people who wear fur garments, as this has not proved to be a successful long-term strategy for other organizations in the past. We decided to introduce a project that would encourage those at the forefront of the industry to work with us to put on a high-profile fur-free fashion show and plant-based gala dinner in order to influence public opinion. But even before that, in 2011, we had already held a pilot campaign to sow the seeds and get people thinking about fur, using the fact that 2011 was the Chinese Year of the Rabbit.

At the time, the fur industry in China was booming, as evidenced by one notable attraction on display throughout China—a large billboard of an actress wearing a full-length raccoon-fur coat, with twelve complete fox tails sewn around the bottom of the coat. We used social media to gather information on public opinions and attitudes toward fur, and in 2012 and 2013, we developed a toolkit for environmental groups to use and distribute that contained fact sheets and a press release on the reality of the fur industry—the animal suffering, human health hazards, and environmental damage. In 2013, we also introduced a national campaign to help university students act through peaceful demonstrations.

Having laid the groundwork and raised awareness over three years, we were ready to take the next step, and our first fur-free fashion show was to be held at a hotel in central Beijing. This was an ambitious endeavor, and as usual, we were operating on a shoestring budget. But the gods smiled on us again: a group of advocates who had staged a fur-free event in their own country of Korea came to support us, bringing faux-fur garments for us to borrow. The pieces, made by brands in Korea, the US, China, and Taiwan, had been exhibited at the show in Korea. (Unfortunately, two days before our show, we were informed by the national security bureau that we would not be permitted to use clothing from the Taiwanese brand.)

We found an agency (pro bono) to handle public relations and promotion via the media to encourage people to attend; they also assigned a stage director to help us and provided free makeup. In determining the presentation style of our show, we emulated the successful annual fashion show by Victoria's Secret, the American lingerie, clothing, and beauty retailer known for its high-visibility marketing and branding. We had four young people sing as the models paraded on the red carpet to display the garments, all in a sort of extravagant "showbiz" style. The venue was classy and ideal for our purposes, and the plant-based buffet for guests of the show was given to us free of charge. After covering the costs of hire, we couldn't afford accommodation at the venue for my colleagues and me, so we opted for a run-down two-star hotel nearby. To transport the garments and display boards to the venue, we had to use a trolley, pushing it across the main road.

In 2015, the following year, we were given space in a large hall in an art gallery in Beijing to put on a similar event—a fur-free fashion show and plant-based buffet. LUSH (the organic cosmetics company) gave us sponsorship, models, and makeup, and we invited the British Embassy to send a representative, which it did.

By 2016, we had worked out how to stage a high-profile event and were excitedly making ambitious plans for the next fashion show. We felt even more excited when Michelle Yeh contacted us, offering to organize the event in Shanghai through her cruelty-free cosmetic company—a wonderful offer that we eagerly accepted. The show was held at the Hyatt Hotel at no cost to ACTAsia and was promoted as a trendy, high-end evening event. LUSH again supported us with models and makeup. We even found sponsorships to cover the costs of the plant-based gala dinner and ended up selling thirty tables with ten seats each. A sponsor all the way from Shenzhen came with one hundred people to our event. Again, the clothes in our show were loaned from fashion houses and displayed by professional models, even accompanied by vegan shoes. We felt that ACTAsia had finally arrived in China, as Shanghai is the capital of the fashion industry in Asia.

I realized that Shanghai, being the global financial and cultural center that it is, was the place to be for ACTAsia to be seen. By chance, Mr. Chang, who had supported the LCA and me during my days in Taiwan, now had an office building in Shanghai and offered ACTAsia some free space that we could use as an office during the two-week fashion show—a most welcome show of his generosity. Then, when his son Peter told me there were many people from Taiwan now living and working in Shanghai, I felt this could be a useful opportunity for fundraising and promoting ACTAsia's work.

Peter offered to introduce me to Yan Zheng Yang, the chairperson of the 1881 Association, a group of Taiwanese ladies aged anywhere between eighteen and eighty-one who were influential charity supporters. Through this connection, I was introduced to Yue Xin Li, a manager at an advertising company and the host of her own radio show, who interviewed me on air for an episode. This further led to my meeting contacts at *ELLE Magazine* and the Rotary Club, both potentially new sponsors.

From 2017, ACTAsia has rented an office in Mr. Chang's Apollo Building. Today, the 1881 Association and Brenda Yang, the current chairperson, continue to be supportive of us, paying for two staff salaries plus office costs. Their support and generosity have given a new dimension to ACTAsia's work in China. The 1881 Association has its own annual gala event and donates the proceeds to four groups, one being ACTAsia.

2018. Pei giving a presentation on Caring for Life education at an event organized by *ELLE Magazine*.

The year 2020 saw our fur-free fashion show reach a new stage in its development. Each year since 2014, the show has evolved and improved little by little, transforming from an amateur albeit well-received first show into a professional show with fashion houses now contacting us and asking to be part of it. Stella McCartney, owner of the world-famous fashion house of the same name, appeared in a video in support of the project, and LCF participated in the newly added forum taking place after our fashion show. The forum, now an annual event accompanying the show, is a place of convergence where international experts from the fashion world discuss and debate compassion in fashion.

Unfortunately, there was no fashion show in 2021, Shanghai being in lockdown because of the COVID-19 pandemic; in 2022, the event was canceled yet again. ACTAsia will stage an annual fur-free and sustainable fashion festival as soon as the pandemic is declared to be over and the Chinese government allows large groups to gather. ACTAsia is also the representative in China for the Fur Free Retailer Scheme, and thanks to the concerted efforts of different groups, every year, more leading brands are agreeing to stop using animal fur and animal skins in their products.

By 2019, I had a small team of full-time and part-time staff working for ACTAsia, representatives in the UK, the US, China, Australia, and the Netherlands, and an international team of expert advisors. Even our funding that year exceeded expectations, as for the past few years, I had become accustomed to chasing every possible funding lead. I'd lost count of the number of times I'd traveled between the US, China, Australia, and Europe to meet sponsors, which I was unable to do when the pandemic hit. (Although we live in the digital age, nothing can match a face-to-face discussion with a potential funder.) Prior to COVID-19, it seemed as if I was always in transit somewhere, almost every week of the year, while on my infrequent days at home, I was mainly occupied with unpacking, listening to Risa as she updated me on her life at school, food shopping to restock the cupboards and fridge for Ross and Risa, leaving instructions for the coming week, and repacking my suitcase with clean clothes.

For more than a decade, I was at home continuously for six weeks at the longest, usually for much less time. I was practically living the life of a nomad. Having a daughter did not stop me from focusing on my work, as I was determined to show my family, colleagues, and friends that I could successfully balance work and motherhood. Often, women who work in the charity sector, especially in Asian countries, give up their careers to focus on their children. I was not going to fall into this category. In my experience, managing a charity is more than a regular job; it's a lifestyle. There are no start times and cut-off times, unless one has the willpower to enforce such discipline. Even so, when running an international charity and managing across time zones, it is often necessary to work unsociable hours, when the rest of the household is asleep.

After Risa had started school, whenever I was about to go away, I prepared detailed instructions for those looking after her in my absence: where she needed to be, at what time, how she would get there, what she needed to take for gym lessons, and when she needed to eat. I had a phone with me twenty-four hours (other than when it was switched off during flights) in case she needed me.

As Risa grew older, ACTAsia also became more established and expansive; my need to travel increased although I still had to keep to a strict budget. Every time, I tried to purchase the quickest and least expensive flights, but this was complicated as the least expensive route sometimes turned out to be the most time-consuming, and vice versa. A life always jetting around the globe may seem glamorous, but it can be tough both mentally and physically, with much sleep lost. Trying to adjust to regular work and sleep patterns when jetlag kicks in can be difficult as the body and mind become disoriented, with overall physical weakness that can last for several days.

There was one occasion when I suddenly became very ill on a long-haul flight back to the UK from China. Unbeknownst to me, I had contracted influenza A, a highly contagious respiratory virus that could result in death without treatment. On arriving home, I was ill for many days, with a high fever and severe aches and pains. I was admitted to the hospital for a week, then took several more weeks to recover. The doctor said that because of my mental strength and determination, I had pushed my body to its physical limit; I needed to take a healthier approach to life and learn to relax. I knew he was right, but would I change?

My last international trip before the COVID-19 pandemic was in mid-January 2020 and included the cities of Beijing, Shanghai, Taipei, and Hong Kong. In particular, I was in Beijing to receive the Best Charity

Leader Award at the China Charity Festival, held at a conference hall with one thousand invited guests in attendance. At the time, I was so excited to be given this award and for ACTAsia to be recognized, completely unaware of the global calamity that was about to take place.

Just ten days after the awards ceremony, I learned that a new infectious disease had been discovered in Wuhan and that the best way to avoid infection was to wear a mask. Jessica wanted to give me a supply of masks to bring back to the UK, but I just laughed and said: "Of course not. The disease is here in China, not in the UK." She persuaded me to take two masks anyway, one to wear on the plane back to the UK and one as a spare. My return journey included a stopover in Hong Kong, and I was waiting for the late-evening flight back to the UK. It was January 23. I remember the date so clearly because it was Lunar New Year's Eve, the most important day of the year for many Asian people. It's when families get together and celebrate. *Why wasn't I with my Taiwanese family?* I pondered. I think I had been too wrapped up in my work to even register it was Lunar New Year's Eve. Suddenly, I felt homesick, thinking of New Year's Eves with my family in Taiwan in years gone by.

As I waited for my flight, I looked at the TV screen, which was showing a Chinese news program. It was announced that the last train to Wuhan had arrived at 10 p.m. and the city had been sealed. No one would be allowed to enter or leave for an unknown period. What was happening? What did this mean? A few hours later, fifteen more cities had been sealed. I was shocked. I knew something must be seriously wrong and feared that changes to everyday life would almost certainly be imposed on everybody.

Only a few people wore masks on my flight, and when we landed at Heathrow, more than three hundred passengers walked freely through immigration without any health checks. The difference between China's response to the virus and the UK's was sharp. I was relieved to get home to Ross and Risa but upset that I had not been with either them or my Taiwanese family on New Year's Eve—to share dinner on this traditional occasion. I became even more upset when the pandemic took hold, as I knew I would not be able to see my family in Taiwan and China for the foreseeable future.

The Lunar New Year celebrations in Wuhan that year were very different from Lunar New Year celebrations in other parts of the world, with residents being told to stay strictly indoors. No visiting friends or relatives, no shopping, and no going out to cinemas or restaurants. This was an unprecedented experience for Wuhan residents. People who had gone away for New Year celebrations had left their pets at home with auto feeders, thinking they would return in a few days. Animals such as dogs, cats, and rabbits were left unattended for days on end, and though aware of what was going on, the authorities would not make exceptions for residents to return home to attend to their animals. Also neglected were vulnerable and elderly people, some of whom died during the three months of quarantine lasting until April 8. To me, this experience indicates that there is a long way to go before compassion for people and animals is widely understood and practiced in China.

With news of the virus in Wuhan spreading around the world, governments and populations outside of Asia still seemed to think they were immune; it was not until Italy reported a high level of infection among its people, with alarming numbers of hospital admissions and deaths, that we recognized the world was under siege from this unknown virus. International flights were suspended, borders between countries were closed, and other restrictions were imposed as we struggled to discover where the virus had come from and how it could be managed.

Watching the situation become more serious each day increased my concern for the future of ACTAsia. I feared funding would become scarce. All of my time in recent years had been split between different countries managing various projects and motivating staff, reporting to existing donors and seeking new ones, while maintaining relationships with corporate sponsors and building a network of key decision-makers and influencers. Before lockdown, I had also been increasing my own profile through speaking engagements and interviews with the media. Now, all of my plans were on hold as events were canceled one by one. Now, my way of working of relentlessly forging ahead suddenly seemed unfeasible, like it had been taken out of my hands. I was acutely aware that funding would almost certainly become much harder to find, as people all around the world were becoming anxious about the security of their own future.

Three months later, fear of the unknown was seriously affecting me: I had no appetite and hardly slept. I had dropped five kilos in weight. Even my doctor was concerned and suggested I might have stomach cancer. When scans and other tests fortunately showed all was clear, having eliminated this possibility, my doctor diagnosed acute stress and anxiety. As the pandemic worsened, I realized that to get through this period, however long it might be, I must develop a more resilient attitude and change my way of working.

Despite the months of uncertainty and worry, I had to recover my composure and concentrate on assuring my staff, who were understandably anxious, that I would do all I could to keep their jobs secure. I needed to be a true leader during these difficult times. The China office staff, who had become familiar with the lockdown procedures months before their colleagues in the UK, had already started doing online lessons for schools and online training for the teachers. It was now apparent that to continue working, we had to quickly adapt and learn how to use online platforms such as Zoom and Microsoft Teams.

Although the source of the new disease was unknown, the main theory pointed toward the transmission of a mutated virus from an animal to a human at a "wet market" in Wuhan. Another theory claimed that the virus had escaped from a laboratory. Various other theories continued to be suggested as an investigation by the WHO yielded no conclusive answers. But while the world was just now turning its attention to the so-called wet markets, where different species of live and dead animals—including fish, fowl, reptiles, birds, mammals, as well as wild animals such as raccoons—were on sale alongside vegetables, fruit, and spices, environmentalists, animal welfarists, and human health authorities had been concerned about these places for many years. Markets of this type can be found in most towns in China and in many Asian countries, and the potential for zoonoses is a real threat given the inadequate health and safety standards, driven by little concern for and understanding of the risks to the public, the animals, and the environment.

To maintain the momentum of ACTAsia's work, we organized online training sessions for veterinarians in China, with emphasis on fur farming, an issue that was now gaining global attention as one theory suggested that mink and other animals farmed for their furs could be intermediate hosts for the coronavirus. ACTAsia's solid research, with reports and data on the Chinese and global fur trades, was widely shared by major media outlets including *CNN*, *BBC*, *Deutsche Welle*, and *Vogue Business*.

I decided that the public health implications of wild animal farming, in general and specifically in the case of zoonotic diseases, could be a topic for useful online debate and discussion, so ACTAsia planned a series of five webinars on the commercial captive breeding of wild animals as well as the illegal wildlife trade in China. Our webinar series was timely, especially given its relevance in the debate about the origins of the coronavirus. A further series explored how we could avoid future pandemics by teaching children, professionals, and consumers worldwide to recognize the interconnection between humans, animals, and the environment. We invited experts from various organizations including One Health in China and the US as well as the WHO to give presentations.

The One Health approach recognizes the well-being of humans, that of domesticated and wild animals, that of plants, and that of the wider environment (including ecosystems) as interlinked and interdependent. As such, I also came to the realization that no one person or organization could work alone in this new world. Though I had always believed that collaboration could be beneficial, in the past, I had been wary of joining coalitions and alliances, thinking of them as little more than talking shops. Now, I decided we needed to align more closely with other organizations, especially environmental groups.

During this time, I was also invited to attend an online webinar hosted by a group called EndPandemics that became a space for intense, stimulating discussion on topics such as possible origins of the virus, the illegal wildlife trade, sea pollution, and pesticides in agriculture. The experts—scientists, businessmen, and environmentalists—were in attendance to offer their opinions, and I myself was invited onto the committee to represent China's perspective. I came away from having attended several sessions with a better understanding of the various topics covered.

COVID-19 has taught us that we can no longer take animals and the environment for granted to use or misuse as we choose, that we can no longer behave as we did toward each other. As for me, the pandemic has only strengthened my commitment to creating a compassionate world for humans, animals, and the environment. Although it has been a painful and difficult experience for many people across the globe, COVID-19 may have been the sharp lesson that the world needed.

Fortunately, at ACTAsia, we found a way to carry on through the pandemic and even emerged from it with new, exciting alliances with other organizations. Although our income was already lower than in previous years, we cut our running costs where we could. Our survival strategy worked. By saving on the budget we had allocated for international travel and not replacing short-term contract employees, we managed to retain every one of our staff and, thankfully, pass through two very dark years relatively unscathed. I have learned that a crisis necessitates careful consideration and calm leadership guided by focus and determination, but the sleepless nights, fears, stress, and tears are still vivid in my mind—I hope we never have to live through another pandemic.

The One Health concept is not new, but it has become better understood in recent years, and its recognition that the health of people is closely connected to the health of animals and our shared environment has been made ever more poignant since the pandemic. As human populations move into new geographical areas, as deforestation and harmful farming practices continue to accelerate climate change, and we face an unprecedented global movement of people, animals, and animal products, all these factors are bringing us into closer contact with animals and their habitats. The implications of this are manifold, not the least of which is that every year, millions of people and animals around the world are affected by zoonotic diseases.

The One Health pathway shows us that the fates of people, animals, and the environment are far from separate but intertwined. Moving forward, I aim to be ever mindful of this important principle when planning ACTAsia's projects and activities. As my journey continues and more challenges arise along the way, regular reviews of all our work and much self-reflection are needed, and above all, a positive mindset. I am confident that these personal observations provide the key to managing and surviving crises ACTAsia and I must face in the future.

Chapter 14

Relaxation: Music and Nature

I'm often asked if I ever relax: my friends describe me as a whirlwind, always rushing, doing something, never switching off. Until recent years, I think my answer would have been, "Rarely." But I am now becoming more aware of the numerous benefits that relaxation brings to human health and well-being. As a child, I never heard anyone in my family talk about relaxing; life was all about surviving. The closest to a vacation for my mother, my siblings, and me was an annual day trip to visit relatives; far from relaxing, the train journey was very exciting for us, taking us into the rural parts of Taiwan that were so different from our busy, bustling, noisy hometown of Taipei.

Each year, my school organized an end-of-year treat, usually a visit to the soy sauce factory to see how the product was made and poured into bottles. Again, my classmates and I were too bouncy about being outside of school for this to be a relaxing activity, though it was a welcome change from our daily routine. Nowadays, people talk about going on vacation when they need to relax, but until I was in my thirties, I had never experienced nor understood real relaxation.

After finishing college, I started to go on hiking trips with my Buddhist friends to the mountainous areas of Taiwan, far away from the hustle and bustle of city life. The group usually consisted of Wu Hung, Asir, Sarah, me, and sometimes my first sister. The purpose of these trips was to experience and absorb the hidden mystery of the natural environment, its beauty and scents—the peace and tranquility during good weather and the angry forces of nature during a storm. Until then, I had very much been a city girl. I knew little about the natural environment, but as living with nature was the central focus of my Buddhist studies, I wanted to experience it firsthand.

In Buddhism, the concept of a natural environment comes from the teachings of Buddha, including that we should treat the natural environment with great care as it is vital for our existence, that spending time close to nature is the ideal way to rebalance our bodies and minds, which can lead to improved concentration and eventual enlightenment, that every one of us has the potential to achieve enlightenment, a physical and mental state wherein spiritual insight into our lives gives us understanding, ethical discipline, wisdom, and emotional balance—freedom from negative feelings of anger, greed, hate, and jealousy. It seems an almost impossible goal, but to aim in that direction is to give greater meaning to our lives.

1990. Hiking with Sarah.

For my first hiking venture, I went to the scenic Dasyueshan National Forest in the Heping District of Taichung to climb Mount Daxue, which was 3,500 meters at its peak. Some of the area had been used for logging in the past but had now been reforested and become a popular destination for birdwatching. Before going, I had to exercise and train for both physical and mental strength by carrying twenty kilos on my back, first for short distances, then gradually building up to longer intervals; I needed to be strong and resilient. We set off at the foot of the mountain in silence, with essential equipment on our backs, ready to endure whatever we encountered. Buddhists believe that silence has the capacity to strengthen spirituality.

I tried to concentrate on the surroundings, but after a while, I found the endless silence (other than the sound of a foot slipping or an occasional gasp) rather boring. The hours ticked by. As we climbed further up the mountain, the air became thinner, with less oxygen. I gradually felt my heart starting to pound and my breathing becoming difficult. It was getting dark and cold. My feet felt heavy and my vision became blurred. Suddenly, I fainted. The next thing I remember is being carried down the mountain by a team of specialist climbers who patrolled the area to rescue people in trouble. I was taken to a hut where I was treated for acute mountain sickness; thankfully, with fluids and medication, within a couple of hours, I was feeling much better.

Despite a rough first experience, my subsequent hiking trips went much better, and I often felt a sense of freedom and of being at peace with myself as we walked in silence in the mountains, though not always. Sometimes, the silence led me to darker places in my mind where I would relive some of the traumas from my earlier life, and on cloudy days, I would feel as if the mountains were alive and threatening me. On other occasions, I became aware of changes in color and density in the scenery while walking from the lower to the

1992. Hiking with LCA colleagues.

higher parts of a mountain, changes that provoked a sense of curiosity and made me question how it was that plants and animals could survive and even thrive in such harsh climatic conditions. Overall, I didn't find hiking to be a relaxing activity, but at times, when the weather was bright and sunny, I did feel some sense of wellness and calm, although such feelings tended to be short-lived.

What did allow me to relax, albeit for short periods of time, were the Buddhist practices of meditation and yoga, which I still practice regularly. Then, I eventually found a sustainable, long-lasting state of calm and relaxation through practical activities, namely flower arrangement and pottery. Today, I still find peace and contentment in arranging flowers and foliage in the European and Japanese styles, which I learned at the Christian church's flower-arranging course some thirty years ago. More than meets the eye, a flower arrangement can take on spiritual and artistic meanings depending on the practitioner, as with the Japanese art of *Ikebana*. I have learned to appreciate all the varied shades of green, red, yellow, and even brown in nature, in the trees, leaves, and flowers. I can also appreciate the varied scents of different types of flowers and plants, as well as the varied textures of different leaves and petals. I found these senses within me to be as enchanting as the finished, elaborate artistic displays. To me, this discovery is ever new. Likewise, my love of ceramics has grown over the years. With ceramics, I can create anything I want from a simple lump of clay, with just an idea, along with some persistence and patience. The finished product may not be beautiful or even what was originally intended, but it still has meaning for me, the creator. I liken ACTAsia to my lump of clay that I have molded from nothing more than a vision, with much persistence and patience along the way.

February 2017 marked Ross's sixtieth birthday, my fiftieth birthday, and Risa's tenth birthday. We decided that for this occasion, we would celebrate with a special holiday together in the Maldives, a country famous for its white-sand beaches and pristine lagoons, with crystal-clear water and extensive coral reefs. The Maldives consists of a chain of more than 1,000 coral islands in the Indian Ocean, only about 2,000 of which are inhabited. As rising sea levels due to climate change pose serious threats to many island countries, there are concerns that the Maldives, too, with many of its islands being less than one meter above sea level, will eventually flood and sink.

On this holiday, I wanted to learn how to dive so I could see life underwater. I wasn't a particularly strong swimmer: I once taught myself how to swim at a pool in Taiwan when I was eleven years old and afterward had little further experience. But after taking part in an investigative project on sea turtles in Bali, I wanted to see these ancient creatures in their natural habitat and observe their behavior. The oldest known sea turtle fossil is at least 120 million years old, meaning sea turtles lived alongside dinosaurs, who became extinct around 65 million years ago; this makes them some of the oldest creatures on the planet. Yet, in the past hundred years, demand for sea turtles' meat, eggs, skin, and colorful shells has drastically reduced their populations. The Turtle Conservancy warns that the destruction of feeding and nesting habitats and the pollution of the world's oceans are both taking a serious toll on the remaining sea turtles. Many breeding populations have already become extinct, and entire species are being wiped out. There could be a time in the near future when sea turtles are just an oddity, found only in aquariums and natural history museums. Currently, six of the seven sea turtle species are classified as threatened or endangered due to human actions and lifestyles. The last of the species, the flatback sea turtle, remains to be classified once further studies and data are available.

I took my first diving lesson with a mixture of emotions and a ringing question: Was it ethically right to invade the home of so many creatures? I wasn't sure, but I was too keen to see life under the sea. I was not disappointed. That trip to the Maldives marked one of the most powerful experiences in my life as I discovered another world underwater. I saw coral reefs, vastly varied in size and color as they were, in yellow, cream, and bluey green. Some resembled stone boulders; others had a softer appearance, like a beautiful garden. Equally magical were the radiant and bright colors of the fish darting all around. I later learned that some 700 species of fish live in those waters, some taking up permanent residence in the coral reefs and others visiting for food.

The highlight of our holiday was an unexpected sighting of a whale shark gliding in the same stretch of water where Ross and I were. I was terrified: he looked enormous, measuring at least twelve meters in length. Eventually, he took no notice of us as he swam by. My diving instructor had told me that we might be lucky enough to see a whale shark; he told me not to be afraid if this should happen but just to enjoy the experience, as there had not been any case anywhere in the world of a whale shark attacking a person. Known as gentle giants, these magnificent creatures feed on plankton and tiny fish and are easily identifiable by their white spots. Sharing a space with a member of this endangered species—such an awe-inspiring colossus—was a great privilege; it made me feel small and insignificant, and it made me marvel at the wonders of the natural world.

Later that day, back on dry land, I was able to recall what I had experienced. I felt sad and ashamed that humans continued to exploit the creatures I had encountered—the turtles, the whale sharks, and the coral reefs. I formed an immediate affinity for diving, and witnessing all the beauty and freedom in the warm waters was the most relaxing and calming experience I had ever known—this relaxing and calming effect didn't stop once I was out of the water. The wonderment and awe induced by this other world I got to experience has stayed uppermost in my mind, helping me put into perspective the pressures, many self-imposed, of everyday life, insignificant as some of them really are.

These incredibly rich experiences notwithstanding, learning to relax at home is another feat. From an early age, I have enjoyed listening to Chinese opera, in which there are regional variations in style and costume, and yet many similarities in the types of roles played by performers and the acting. When I came to the UK, I found Western opera to be not so different in terms of the storylines; it only sounded different because of the particularities of Western instruments and music. Now, I listen to Puccini's *La Bohème*, one of the most famous operas ever written and a favorite of mine, repeatedly, especially while driving long-distance. I have always found that orchestral sounds, the cello in particular, stir up emotions from deep down inside of me. That said, I enjoy most types of classical music, which I find motivating when I am working. When driving in my car,

I usually listen to classical music by artists such as Andrea Bocelli, the world-famous operatic tenor, whose soothing voice helps me to relax.

I would have loved to learn to dance as a child, but we had no money for dance classes. To me, music and dance represent a type of freedom. I am now learning to play the piano in a continued effort to relax more and free myself of negative thoughts.

I've never been inclined to explore the more "fun" hobbies such as chess, card games, or physical sports, but I am thankful that I can find peace in nature and music. I am also thankful that so much of my Buddhist training has sustained me through the years. Meditation and yoga always have a place in my daily schedule, and I am comforted by the sayings of Buddha, especially this: *"Accept what is. Let go of what was. Have faith in what will be."*

Chapter 15

Tiger Mother

From my early twenties, I had been adamant that I did not want to have children. I thought it was selfish to bring a child into the world because a child had no choice regarding its birth. I also thought the main reason for having a child (and a wrong one at that) was for the benefit of the parents, to make sure there would be someone to take care of them in their old age. My friends and siblings were convinced I was anti-children; they were as sure as I was that I would never have a child of my own.

When I was small, my mother was so busy trying to earn money to feed the family that her parenting style was inevitably different from those of mothers who were able to devote more time to their children. Then, the loss of both my father and my mother, one when I was a child and the other when I was a young teenager, meant that I had no parental role model in my life. I didn't have an adult to turn to when I was worried or afraid or to ask questions about life, someone who would care for me when life became difficult or console me when I felt desperate. I had no one to tell me that everything was going to be all right even as I went through stormy periods in life.

I never had the opportunity to learn and appreciate the value of family or the joy of being a mother—the pleasure of giving and receiving unconditional love. So I just never had any plans that included children.

The first time I became pregnant, I was in a controlling and toxic relationship. The pregnancy was unplanned: I knew that at some stage, I needed to escape but that I would never be able to leave him if we had a child. Unable to admit that I was in a dangerous relationship, I never told any of my friends or family. When I miscarried, my miscarriage brought sadness but also relief. Even so, I carried memories of the unwanted baby for many years with a heavy heart, with feelings of guilt and inadequacy, trying hard to move forward.

Years later, when I knew I had met the right man, I started to have maternal feelings. I could not understand why I was feeling this way, having resolved to never have children. The only reason I could find was that I was approaching middle age and would soon hit forty, that my biological clock was ticking, as the saying goes. But I was now much happier and more content with life than at any time that I could remember. I felt less anxious, more self-aware, and generally more confident. I had now made some friends at work. We freely shared our respective customs and cultural traditions with each other, often going to ethnic restaurants together and celebrating events such as Lunar New Year, Christmas, and Easter. I now found myself able to relax and laugh at some of our cultural differences instead of acting defensively or taking offense as I had tended to do in the past. Ross's family was also warm and welcoming to me. His two brothers and sister had their own children, which made family get-togethers great fun and filled with laughter. So, although I had been subconsciously toying with the possibility of having a child, I was still shocked and bewildered when, at the age of thirty-nine, I realized I was pregnant. It dawned on me soon after I returned from the Pioneer Training residential in Italy in October 2005. Along with this knowledge that I was pregnant, my insecurities immediately came to the fore: *How could I become a mother? Am I capable? Do I have enough love in my heart to be the role model I never had?* Ross, being ten years older than me, already had an adult son and had experienced difficulties raising him. *Would he want to start again with a baby? Would he think he was too old?* When we started to discuss the future, one in which we had not planned to have a child together, both of us found it hard to express in words how we were feeling. As we were about to leave for a holiday, we agreed to discuss all the implications while we were away and make our decision once we were home.

On the last but one day of our holiday, I received the terrible news that Betty Wang, one of the Chinese trainees at our Pioneer Training, had jumped to her death from the balcony of the condominium where she had lived with her husband. I had known and mentored Betty for a few years, helping her with animal welfare issues in China. I will always remember the moment when I heard the devastating news of her death, the moment when the beautiful landscapes of the remote Indonesian island I was on seemed to fade into nothingness. I was in shock and despair: Betty was such a warm, talented person that it was difficult to believe she was no longer in this world.

The next day, soon after checking into a hotel before we were about to head back to the UK, I noticed when using the bathroom that I was bleeding slightly. I thought the emotional stress caused by the tragic news about Betty and the turbulent waves hitting against the small boat we had been on had disturbed the fetus, so I stayed in bed to rest until it was time to board our flight home. On arriving home, I was still bleeding, more heavily now. I went to the hospital, where the doctor confirmed I was having a miscarriage.

I remember crying almost nonstop for days, then weeks, then months; I felt disconnected from all that was happening around me. Even as Christmas was approaching, I felt numb and could not bother with the happy expectations that accompanied the festive season. During the post-miscarriage check-up, I broke down in floods of tears at the doctor's clinic. I was told that I had postnatal depression even though I hadn't given birth.

The incident alarmed Ross, who wanted to know how he could help me; to his surprise, I said I wanted to go and stay with his parents, who lived in a tiny cottage in a remote part of Wales. I was not particularly close to them. He could not understand my thinking, and I couldn't explain why I wanted to go either, but I insisted on going—alone. Only later, once my thought process was back on track, did I realize what had happened at that time: I was missing my mother so much that all I wanted was to feel some parental love, even if not from my own parents.

Six months later, in May 2006, I decided to go to China, one of my purposes being to visit Betty's family. Having just emerged from a dark period myself, I also wanted to talk to the Chinese animal welfare groups and the volunteers she had worked with and remind them of the importance of self-care, a topic fresh in my mind. During my brief retreat in Wales, Ross's parents had given me plenty of time and space to meditate and process the past few months. I had decided that I wanted to set up a new organization, the type of organization that was different and needed in Asia, one whose philosophy was not based solely on emotion but was outward-looking, with holistic aims centered on the well-being of society.

With these ideas for a new organization at the forefront of my mind, I also used my time in China to visit contacts in Shenzhen, Beijing, and Changsha to test the waters. The response I got was encouraging; I felt enthused and ready for the next steps. I did some initial planning with several fledgling animal protection groups and knew I could play a useful role in China, coordinating their actions. But toward the end of the trip, I began to feel unwell. Tired and dizzy, I wondered if I was developing a cold or had perhaps eaten some badly prepared food. To my amazement, I soon realized I was pregnant again! The journey from China back to the UK was like a strange dream to me, having spent the past couple of weeks excitedly forming the foundations of a new organization and carving out a demanding timetable for the coming year. And now I was pregnant—again?

Once I was home, the old feelings of inadequacy overtook rational thinking. I felt as if my life was one long roller coaster. Could I learn to become a loving mother? Was I even capable of being one? Was I mentally strong enough to cope with whatever life would throw at me in the future? Surprisingly, Ross warmed to the idea of becoming a father again, although it would be later in life than he had ever anticipated. He assured me we could raise a child in a happy home full of love. He told me I must not doubt myself. My previous miscarriage had left me consumed by grief, but there was no reason why it should happen again. Ross was so positive about our future together as a family that he convinced me. I was determined to become the best mother I could be.

I didn't enjoy being pregnant, which for me meant months of migraines and indigestion. I wanted to look like the glamorous pregnant women featured in magazines, serene and relaxed with their silky hair and soft, blemish-free skin, but instead, I felt fat and exhausted. Regardless, I resolved not to dwell on looks for long. My goal during the forty drudging weeks of pregnancy was to set up the new organization before my baby arrived. ACTAsia for Animals was officially registered as a nonprofit company on January 3, 2007, and I worked up to the point when labor pains took over. I recall the pains starting around 10 p.m. one day as I was frantically trying to finish some outstanding administration matters. My last email was hurriedly sent at 2:20 a.m. to Deepa, the co-founder of ACTAsia, to say that I really was about to have a baby . . . at the age of forty.

The birth process was long and traumatic, culminating with a forceps delivery and blood transfusion, a painful and frightening experience. Then, they presented me with this small bundle of life, whom we named Risa, and I thought the difficult times were over. How naïve and wrong I was! I found the first three months of motherhood extremely scary. Every time my baby girl cried, I could feel the panic rising inside me. Each feed was a struggle: I did not have enough breast milk to feed this hungry child, and she couldn't latch on properly. Many times, I silently told myself that I was too old for all this.

I took six weeks off to learn how to bond with Risa, then gradually eased back into work with whatever time I had between the lengthy feeds and other baby duties. When Risa was around six weeks old, I was invited to be the keynote speaker at an animal rights conference in New York. I agreed, reasoning with myself that Risa would be three months old by the conference date; surely, I would have a structured routine in place well before then.

2009. Having fun in the sea with Risa aged 2 years.

Ross and my mother-in-law firmly disagreed with me, saying that it was not a good idea for me to accept the speaking engagement. "Why?" was my response. "Chinese mothers go back to work when their children are one month old; surely, I can go back after three months." I was ignoring the fact that Chinese women do not usually leave their country for work. Still, I was determined to go.

I recall having to pump my breast milk, lest it should disappear, in the toilet at the conference venue and in the organizers' office. I had not told the organizers that I had recently given birth. They were shocked to learn that I had a three-month-old baby 3,500 miles away!

When Risa was five months old, I decided it was time to focus on ACTAsia. I took her to Taiwan to see my family and friends; after settling her into a routine, I left her with my second sister and traveled to China to join my colleague and visit the groups I was getting to know. I felt it was important to find out the type of training they needed in order to help strengthen their capacity, as there was little knowledge or information in China at that time relating to animal welfare. As with my visit to the US, I had to carry on pumping milk throughout the trip. This time, it was more difficult as we were constantly on the move, always in a car or train or on board a domestic flight. On the last day of the trip, I was to travel from Guangzhou to Hong Kong via train. When our train (which was fortunately not crowded) was delayed, I had no choice other than to do what I had to do. Suddenly, an announcement told us that due to a technical issue, we had to get off. As we rushed to leave the train, milk spilled onto the seats and the floor of the carriage. My colleague was horrified, and I wanted to crawl into a hole in the ground to hide my embarrassment.

Risa was born in 2007, the year after ACTAsia became a reality, when I had just one other co-founder and one part-time volunteer fundraiser. We had no money to hire staff, so my days were overflowing as I juggled baby, partner, housework, and new organization. But once Risa passed the three-month milestone, she became a model baby. We had found a routine that worked for all of us in our home, so I was able to sneak in work between her naps and bedtimes. Fortunately, I need only five to six hours of sleep each day and often worked well into the night.

Friends often asked, "Why do you work such long hours when you have a baby?" I think it was probably because I was determined not to be one of the women who would leave nonprofit work after entering a relationship or starting a family. I wanted to prove that in order to have children and a family life, one didn't have to stop being passionate about a cause or making useful contributions to the world.

I traveled regularly to various countries for speaking engagements at meetings and conference and for networking with potential sponsors. To be able to do this, I relied on Ross, a network of friends, and local moms to care for Risa in my absence, leaving detailed daily instructions for them to make sure that her needs were always covered. Then, when the COVID-19 pandemic came in 2020, with lockdown and other restrictions that prevented further travel, I was able to work from home and spend more time with her.

I find that the well-known ancient African proverb, "It takes a village to raise a child," applies to our experience of raising Risa. Indeed, although a child's immediate family does directly shape their personality, values, and beliefs, others in the community play a significant role in ensuring their safety and good overall development. Risa was well cared for in my absence by many people, and I believe it is thanks to this that she has grown into a confident, articulate, and independent sixteen-year-old young lady who shows care and concern for human and animal well-being as well as the environment.

It may seem that having a child made my life more difficult given how focused I had been on my work, but the opposite is true. As I

2021. Risa aged 14 years.

grew as a mother, I became more tolerant of others and stronger, both physically and mentally. I enjoy learning about Risa's school life—both the ups and the downs—and watching her make relationships with her classmates. I have learned so much about myself by looking at life through the eyes of a child and seeing beauty in the simple things, even just walking in the rain and splashing in puddles.

I now also have friends who are not from the charity sector and not particularly vocal about social issues like animal welfare or the environmental crisis, but are happy, kind people, content to be with their children and family. Hearing their perspectives on life has helped me find balance within my own life, and learning about their interests has brought a new, enriching and fulfilling dimension. I can appreciate our differences, in physical appearance and in thought.

I am often told by a colleague that I am naturally defensive and suspicious of people and their intentions. Perhaps I am, and perhaps this is an ingrained cultural trait. But I think I am becoming less so than in the past. At the very least, I know that before becoming a mother, I had viewed life only through a narrow lens, whereas now, I stop to think and try to understand and appreciate others' viewpoints.

Ross and I got married in 2011, when Risa was four years old. Risa has become my sanctuary; caring for her and enjoying time with her are how I recharge. I believe she was a gift from God or Buddha because without her, I would have worked myself to the point of burnout and possibly given up on my mission to create a more compassionate world for all beings.

I learned the meaning of resilience through raising Risa, the same resilience that has allowed me to cope with ACTAsia's lack of staff and funding, as well as the petty problems that arise almost daily in the workplace. I continue to learn how to be a good mother, although I know some may disapprove of my parenting style and label me a "tiger mother," a mother with exceedingly high expectations for her child. I don't have a problem with this label: it is my duty, in alignment with my culture, to ensure that my child works hard. But I also believe that it is vital to let a child know that they are loved unconditionally—something I never knew or experienced in my childhood—in order to have a solid relationship with them, a relationship based on strength, patience, resilience, kindness, and forgiveness. I think of these five qualities as the five elements of parent power (a concept I have introduced to parents in China through a series of presentations and discussions).

So, when asked what my greatest achievement in life is, without hesitation, I answer, "Risa."

TIGER MOTHER
by Risa Dyer

You have a tiger mother
They told me when I was four
I don't understand
I would say

My mummy doesn't walk on four paws
I don't have a tiger mother
She isn't orange
She doesn't run rampant in exotic jungles

You have a tiger mother
I was told
When I was fifteen, I realized
Maybe I did have a tiger mother

Her angry words like a savage growl
Claws coming out to defend me
Strong and fearsome
Brave
Always looking to protect, nurture

I do have a tiger mother
Now, when they tell me
I don't flush under their watchful eyes
I smile proudly
I do have a tiger mother.

Chapter 16

On Reflection

I sometimes wonder what my parents would have thought of my work with ACTAsia. Indeed, if I hadn't lost both of them at such a young age, it is unlikely that I would have worked in the nonprofit sector, as Asian parents strongly discourage their children from taking low or unpaid jobs. Also, having witnessed my mother's struggles, I would probably have wanted to pursue a well-paying career so I could look after her and provide some comfort in her old age. One thing is almost certain, though: it's unlikely that I would have met and married a Western man.

While working on this book, I've realized that even now, forty years after my mother's death, I still miss her deeply. There is buried inside me a young girl in her mid-teens longing for her mother's love. I wish I could give her a tight hug right now and tell her how much I love her in just the same way I repeatedly tell my daughter, although when I was a child, the word "love" was never spoken. I know that the permanent sense of loss has created a large hole in my heart that cannot be filled. My siblings and I never talk about how we each feel about having lost our mother; our wounds leak little by little as we cope with our everyday lives.

I wish I could share my highs and lows with my mother and tell her that she has a beautiful and intelligent albeit headstrong granddaughter. Like many other daughters, I also want to moan to her about my husband and about difficult days at work. I know she would tell me, "Buckle down, listen to your man, and appreciate what you have in life." I know she would be so proud of my achievements and thrilled that I am able to tell my story in this book. I can imagine her saying to her friends that she never thought her youngest daughter, known to the family as Ugly, would have the courage to start a social change organization; she would probably joke that her ugly duckling has finally turned into a beautiful swan.

As for my sisters and brother, they used to wonder what I was doing, as I didn't tell them until afterward that I had created an organization. Later, as they learned more about my work from reading ACTAsia's Chinese website, they became ACTAsia supporters, giving regular donations. This tells me that they approve, even as they are unlikely to say to me, "Well done." I know this will seem strange to Western readers, but it is not in our culture to speak in this way. Still, I know that they are proud of their youngest sister.

I feel fortunate to have grown up in the East, then spent more than half of my life living and working in the West; the diverse cultural, social, and political environments I have been submerged in have enabled me to understand people and events more rationally than I might have done otherwise.

When I left home in my late twenties, I was not really in control of my life—I was drifting. I had been living an insecure life, with periods of depression and despair peppered throughout the years. Now, I know I took the right path when I decided to leave Taiwan. There is not a dearth of cultural platitudes about traumas in life: people say, "Everything happens for a reason," and, "What doesn't kill you makes you stronger." Many may find such sayings trite and lacking in validity, but they do hold some meaning for me. I believe that the challenges of my early life prepared me for the next stages of my journey, and I have emerged from those challenges stronger and more resilient. This may seem a convenient and overly spiritual attitude toward life, but in Buddhist culture, we believe that "suffering is inevitable, therefore acceptable." Strangely enough, when looking back on my younger days, I am almost thankful that the road I walked was as bumpy as it was. Of course, if I could turn the clock back, my mother would still be with me and I would be taking good care of her in her old age, but that can only happen in my dreams.

It has been thirty years since I started working in the animal welfare/humane education movement. In this book, I've tried to analyze the various stages of my life as best I can, with the benefit of hindsight, as well as to reflect on my personal development. As I come to the end of my story and journey thus far, I leave you with the following questions I've posed to myself and my attempts at the most honest and open answers to them.

* * *

Q1. In previous chapters, you've highlighted your negative experiences and the resulting lack of confidence and low self-esteem that troubled you in the past. To what extent are these issues still present in your life?

Less and less in recent years. Back then, I found leaving Taiwan and everything familiar to me a real wrench. I wasn't happy with my life and was aimlessly searching for something—I didn't even know what that something was. I now realize what a huge step it was for me to travel alone from Taiwan to the US and Europe—into the unknown—as there are so many ways in which the East and the West are culturally different, sometimes diametrically opposed. I hadn't anticipated that very simple things could cause me anxiety and fear that I might be laughed at. Take drinking water: In Taiwan, we drink hot water, but in the West, it's usual to have a glass of cold water. If I feel a bit unwell, perhaps from a headache or tummy ache, I would place a cold-water compress on my head, whereas in the West, it is usual to curl up with a water bottle containing hot water. Likewise, books are read from back cover to front cover in my native country; the opposite is true in the UK. So knowing I was different made me feel very self-conscious in the early days, and although I tried hard to appear confident, I often felt like a scared rabbit caught in the headlights.

Over time, however, I have developed more confidence and largely overcome my low self-esteem. People who know me only from recent years will probably be surprised (and amused) to learn that I ever struggled with my self-esteem, but I still need to work on being more assertive, especially when managing a growing organization.

Q2. When you first worked in the UK, colleagues often found you abrupt and unfriendly. Why?

I think it was mainly due to my being anxious and feeling like a bit of a fraud! I had been away from Taiwan for just four years when I started working at the WSPA; during those four years, I had been in the US gaining some work experience, then in London for language school, then at university in Essex. So when I was suddenly put in the workplace and onto a team, I had no experience to draw on and had to learn how to become a good actress very quickly. It was a new world for me, and I was immediately thrust into the fast-moving pace of the organization with little supervision. Often, I simply didn't understand what was being said to me; rather than admit this, I would either say nothing or perhaps act indifferent. I was in awe of my colleagues, who seemed to know so much about the many issues we were working on, so I avoided joining conversations in which my lack of knowledge might be exposed.

Although I was hired specifically to advise on lifestyles and attitudes in Asian societies, I was expected to fill many other roles. For example, soon after I joined the WSPA as Project Officer for Asia,

I was tasked with coordinating 350 animal welfare groups that were the WSPA's member societies. This was a huge undertaking, and it now seems almost crazy that I had only ever worked as a volunteer for one NGO yet was expected to help and advise NGOs in countries from those of the Pacific Islands to Canada, from South Africa to Mongolia. Why was I asked to do this job and why did I say yes?

Although I attended an English language school in London for three months, then even managed to get a master's degree, this was not enough for me to speak proficiently, and my vocabulary was quite limited. In the Chinese language, words, including verbs, typically have just one grammatical form each and always stay the same, whereas in English, verbs usually change according to the subject and tense. My spare time was dedicated to tackling English grammar; I spent hours and hours on my own with my dictionary and thesaurus, learning new words and trying to improve my understanding of the language just a little more each day.

My being Chinese, people assumed that I knew all about animal welfare in China. In fact, I knew very little: China was not yet open to the rest of the world. Thankfully, I was in regular contact with Wu Hung and my former colleagues from EAST, so I was able to count on their knowledge and expertise to help me through some difficult days. But although the first few months in my new work environment in the UK were challenging, I realized that I learn very quickly and retain information well. Within a year, I had grown in confidence; I was able to do my job well, advising colleagues on the intricacies of Chinese society and politics. It certainly helped that I was a convincing actress!

Cultural differences are very real and can easily lead to misunderstandings. I wanted to be friendly with my colleagues but was frightened of making mistakes. Many of us from Asian cultures do not like to make mistakes as it suggests vulnerability, so we tend to keep silent. Also, my English friends tell me that they find Asian people tend to maintain neutral facial expressions and had difficulties gauging how I was feeling or what I was thinking, whereas Westerners tend to be far more expressive and often show it in their faces if they're annoyed, scared, happy, or sad.

Q3. Having worked with a grassroots organization in Taiwan and a global organization based in the UK, did you experience any major differences?

The most significant difference between Asian and Western cultures that I've experienced, generally speaking, is summed up by the opposing concepts of collectivism versus individualism—the cultural ethos that has been embedded into the social structure of a place, depending on the dominant values and principles. In many Asian countries, mainly those with authoritarian governments and especially those influenced by Confucianism, we are taught that the needs of the group (a company, organization, or business) are of greater importance than those of the individual, that we must work hard for the greater good of all while giving minor consideration to ourselves. This is in marked contrast to Western countries, which value personal choice and prioritize or at least give equal consideration to the individual's concerns and needs.

When I became a manager at the WSPA, I was mystified as to why I was expected to continuously show my appreciation to individual colleagues by saying "thank you" and giving positive feedback. I understand now, but at the time, I had no idea that how the Western workplace functioned was opposite to what I had experienced in Taiwan. In international work, it is entirely possible to overlook the social structure of a target country and the mentality of its population in the planning process. I think important cultural differences like that between collectivist and individualist mindsets should be carefully addressed whenever an organization is planning projects abroad or working with an international staff.

On reflection, I wish I had been aware of this cultural divide from the beginning of my time working in the UK, as I would have made a conscious effort to acclimate to the norms of my workplace. I would have been able to settle into the job and make friends more easily without misunderstandings, and I would not have been labeled as rude or indifferent. I don't think the size or type of an organization, whether it is a grassroots or global organization, is the deciding factor, but it is an understanding of the particularities of the workplace culture that can make or mar one's experience.

Q4. Did you experience any form of racialized prejudice toward you, either in the US or in Europe?

Yes, often . . . I believe that prejudice is inbuilt in all of us humans: regardless of where we originate from, it seems to be universal. When we look at people who wear different clothes, speak different languages, and eat different foods from ours, we naturally compare and judge. Prejudice can develop without our realizing it, perhaps due to a lack of empathy, or perhaps due to historical forces or influence from the media. But regardless of how and why it occurs, when one experiences any form of prejudice, it is hurtful. Our children must be taught to treat all members of the human race, irrespective of origins, as they themselves would want to be treated.

In my experience, racial prejudice is more visible in China and other Asian countries and more covert in Europe. For example, in China, many still openly hold the belief that black people are inferior to Chinese people, that they are unintelligent, smelly, noisy, and unfaithful to their partners. Parents would be horrified if one of their children had a relationship with a black person. On the other hand, in European countries, mixed-race families are a normal and accepted part of a diverse populace.

Like I said, I found racism in the UK subtler than in Asia; racist attitudes may not always be verbally expressed, but perhaps a look or facial expression is a giveaway. Today, after having lived in Europe for many years, I still occasionally sense some glances of disdain from complete strangers, and I still feel conscious of being a foreigner. When Ross and I came to live in this typical British suburban village, some people either ignored me or rarely spoke to me for about six years; when we were out walking together, I always felt that I was seen as his mail-order bride.

When Risa was about to start kindergarten, I told Ross that we should get married sooner rather than later. I did not want our child to be the only mixed-race child at kindergarten who had been born outside of marriage; I felt that she would be disadvantaged—labeled as an oddity, maybe even bullied. So Ross and I married in July, just before Risa was due to start school in September. As for me, despite my experiences of being on the receiving end of racial prejudice, I tried hard to adapt to the English way of living. I started cooking a roast dinner every Sunday and even learned how to bake apple pie and make custard!

Q5. Did you think you would settle in the UK or was it just a useful stepping stone at the time?

I originally just wanted to find out what was beyond the borders of Taiwan and had no firm plans for the length of time I would be away. At times, I longed for the sights and smells of my home country, such as the sweet, lightly spiced scent coming from the numerous food stalls that lined the streets. Strangely enough, I missed the hustle and bustle of the crowded streets, the loud engine noises and hooting coming from the seemingly endless stream of mopeds weaving through the chaotic traffic. I missed having conversations with my friends and former colleagues, people with whom I could communicate without having to consult my electronic translator or having to construct sentences in my mind before trying to speak. I even missed the hot, steamy weather, as I found the long periods of cold, rainy days in London rather depressing. And above all, I missed my sisters, with whom I could speak freely and gossip about family life. They regularly sent me food parcels and came to London once a year to see me, bringing still more food and new clothes for me. We have now gone on some great holidays together, especially in France; on one occasion, Princess Elisabeth de Croÿ actually arranged for us to stay in a beautiful chateau in Burgundy, about five miles from her own home. We were so excited—we felt like Disney princesses. I'm glad that my leaving Taiwan has given all of my family new experiences and a different perspective on the world.

I will also say that after spending so much time away from Asia during the COVID-19 pandemic, I started to miss the efficiency and convenience of day-to-day life there, where people seem to be more willing to do a job quickly, even if they have to go out of their way to do it. For example, if I need some printing or artwork done on short notice, I would send it to China and it would get done overnight, whereas in the UK, "short notice" usually means at least one week.

Being married to Ross, and now with Risa in school, I divide my time between Asia and the UK. I feel settled, but my homeland does sometimes seem to be summoning me back.

Q6. What was your main reason for starting ACTAsia?

Mainly my frustration with large organizations as I got to know them more and more. I may have misunderstood, but it seemed to me as if these organizations saw themselves as almost more important than their cause. I perceived something of an attitude of superiority. Although there was a THINK GLOBAL, ACT LOCAL sign clearly displayed in my workplace, it seemed nothing more than a simple slogan, as we spent little time on getting to know the cultures of the countries we were working in. I know it is not a popular statement, but this was how I felt at the time, and I was not exactly alone. In my role as coordinator of the WSPA's member societies, I was able to find out that the opinions of many local groups—especially smaller ones—in different countries were in line with my own observations.

It is difficult for those living in an established democracy to grasp the day-to-day challenges of working in an authoritarian country with limited freedom of speech and a civic society still in its infancy. So when well-meaning Westerners with little to no first-hand experience of Asian countries seemed reluctant to listen to the views and opinions of local groups in those same countries, I found this most disrespectful.

Today, I believe the animal welfare movement is slightly better in this regard. But at the time, I felt that I could set up an organization that would better serve the needs of local groups. Staying true to that mission, for all of ACTAsia's projects, we continue to use the Train the Trainers model, which can be adapted by local groups to suit their needs and cultures.

Q7. How did you plan to attract funding?

I naïvely thought that if I could show ACTAsia was professionally managed and had solid, workable plans, money would come in. I was wrong. Small amounts—one to five thousand pounds—dribbled in, but often with the caveat that the money could not go toward core costs such as salaries. It's an outdated opinion that people who work for a charity should either be volunteers or earn low wages. UK charity law states that a charity should be run as a business: how, if there is no machinery for generating sufficient funding? It's a catch-22 situation: low income equals limited work; limited work equals low income. For the first nine years, the small core group of volunteers at ACTAsia was not paid; even consultants would be reimbursed only for travel expenses. Funding for our work in China was sourced from trust funds and a small nucleus of supporters in the Netherlands, thanks to Nel van Amerongen, our volunteer fundraiser.

Fundraising in the nonprofit sector in the US, UK, and elsewhere in Europe is extremely competitive, with droves of organizations competing for a slice of the pie. And while large organizations can employ teams of marketing and communications professionals to promote their cause at every opportunity, small and medium organizations cannot afford such luxury. ACTAsia is at the stage where we must find a way to attract major donors who share our vision of using education to combat human greed and the cognitive dissonance that are at the root of so much suffering, thereby making room for compassion. My aim is for ACTAsia to become financially sustainable long-term, with more full-time professional employees. This will enable us to expand our reach and tackle issues that affect people, animals, and the environment more effectively and efficiently.

Q8. Have there been times when you thought about disbanding the charity? If so, why?

Yes, there have been many times over the years when I questioned whether we could, or even should, continue—numerous days when

I doubted that I had the ability to lead a well-run organization. But after a few sleepless nights and hours of wrestling between my sensible self and demoralized self, I would bounce back. If only there were a startup fund available to charities so that a small team of about three people could be salaried from the onset; it would be tremendously helpful in relieving the worry of insufficient income. The standard of work at ACTAsia has always been high, thanks to professionals who have volunteered their time and expertise to help us, but retaining staff is always a concern. With all the pressures of modern-day living, it is not reasonable to expect employees to work for low wages, with no benefits such as pension or health insurance. Unfortunately, seeking support for humane education work has become almost a mission impossible, despite it being the most effective solution for long-term social change, as people tend to look for quick fixes rather than address root causes.

The lockdown periods caused by the pandemic were very dark days for me, thinking ACTAsia could collapse. Then, I suddenly realized that ACTAsia is one of the organizations on the front line: we could use the situation to our advantage. Contrary to our fears that we would be sitting around with little to do, we were as busy as ever, perhaps even more so, and we carried on with our mission of raising awareness of the interrelatedness of people, animals, and the environment.

My journey with ACTAsia has never been easy; even now, I still have days when I feel like I am floundering at the bottom of a well, but then I manage to see the light shining at the top, which motivates me to climb back up and continue the battle. Funding is still a constant headache, but fortunately, ACTAsia is now in a stronger financial position thanks to greater marketing strategies during the past five years. I mentioned in Chapter 11 that John Ruane, CEO of Naturewatch, once told me it would take ten to fifteen years to start to see a regular stream of funding. At the time, I thought he was exaggerating, but it has taken us even longer—ACTAsia is now seventeen years old!

Q9. How has the way you manage people changed?

I know I am a hard taskmaster and perhaps more demanding at times than is reasonable. I am also told that instead of micro-managing, I need to delegate more work and responsibility to capable colleagues than I do at present. I come from Taiwan, where the workplace is vastly different from that in the UK, so I understand my management style does not appeal to everyone, and from time to time, as in every walk of life, there may be some friction. Once aware of such friction, I try to deal with it at the earliest opportunity. But especially now, since we all work from home, we sometimes encounter difficulties that could more easily be addressed if we worked together in an office.

I hope I am gradually becoming more understanding and tolerant, especially now that I see how important it is to ensure ACTAsia has a sustainable future so that the time and effort we have put into it will not be in vain. Staff retention is incredibly important, and if we do not invest in training and managing staff members—providing reasonable salaries and working conditions, being understanding of their personal situations, showing appreciation for their efforts—we pay a much higher price.

I do realize that I'm incredibly fortunate that at various points of my journey, I have had help and guidance from the right people at the right time, and that each achievement along the way, however small, has helped me to believe in myself. Playing the role of CEO can be a lonely undertaking as one is expected to have all the answers and sleepless nights seem to be par for the course, and as a leader, one must be careful about showing vulnerability as it can erode confidence and demotivate others. Nonetheless, I am learning to be more compassionate toward myself as well as others, to rest more and to accept that the world will not collapse if I sleep seven to eight hours at night instead of five to six hours.

This may sound trivial, but it's a lesson I've learned. Compassion toward ourselves and others is essential when we face the unprecedented challenges of today's world.

Q10. What are your strengths and weaknesses?

I consider my strengths to be that I'm extremely hardworking, resilient, and good at seizing opportunities and making things happen—I believe strongly in ACTAsia's mission and increasingly in myself. I often remind myself that I am a visionary and that I'm fortunate to pursue work that helps to create a more compassionate world through education. I have a purpose in life and the determination to make it a reality.

I am told that my weaknesses include trying to do too much, being a control freak who is never satisfied, not always acknowledging the contributions of others, and expecting people to work as hard as I do. Do I accept that these are my weaknesses? Perhaps in part, but I am working on getting better. I do accept that from time to time, I become overtired and overreact to minor matters—I'm working on that too. I also have a good sounding board in Ross: if I'm being difficult or unreasonable, he would immediately let me know.

Q11. What are the key factors that drive you on?

Many Asian countries have developed education systems that turn children into academic machines who retain vast amounts of information from their studies but tend to emerge lacking emotional intelligence. Yet, without developing critical thinking skills, they cannot transform the information they learn into knowledge and power. Despite the fact that Asia has the highest number of PhD and master's graduates, sadly, many still don't have a good understanding of responsible citizenship, and some people in leadership positions have a lot of academic credentials yet promote conflict and violence. This is why I believe that Caring for Life education holds the key to solving twenty-first–century issues and that the six-year course is just as important as math, science, and languages. Through CFL education, children can learn how to become responsible global citizens, and as they grow up, they can form their own opinions instead of being overly influenced by their peers and social media.

During the past ten years, ACTAsia's training programs in China have steadily produced greater and greater results. This shows that a small organization can make a difference. To date, more than 350,000 children have received CFL education in schools and community

2017. Children at the Caring for Life education summer camp in a rural area.

centers; more than 4,000 veterinarians have been trained; and our Compassion in Fashion show and forum continue to reach 50 million people each year through various media outlets. It is often said that success breeds success; this certainly applies to ACTAsia.

Ross supported me and ACTAsia financially for the first ten years; although he thought I was crazy in the early days, working so hard with no salary, he can now see the potential value to society of this work. The numerous accolades that ACTAsia and I have received from the business sector, government departments in China, and most notably, the United Nations show him that his support and tolerance have enabled me and my colleagues to create something worthwhile.

Despite the everyday battles and challenges, every small step or achievement has motivated me to keep going and be grateful for the opportunity I have to make the world a better place for the next generation.

Q12. In what ways has the time you've devoted to ACTAsia affected your personal life?

I would like to say that it has made no difference, but I know that is not strictly true. There have been countless times when Ross had no meals ready for him because I either was away or had been working nonstop all day. I rarely go to bed before about 3 a.m. and regularly have Skype calls during the night owing to the time differences between the UK and Asian countries. As Ross gets up around 5 a.m. to head off to London for his work, our time together is limited. This arrangement is not ideal, but we have nonetheless learned to make it work for us. It gets far more complicated when young children are involved. Risa often had to stay with different people whenever I was away. On one occasion, she said to me, "I feel like a parcel; I am always being passed around."

2016. Caring for Life education class for some of China's 'left behind children.'

When Risa was about six years old and about to take her first violin examination, I had to leave for China, and so Joy was staying over and took Risa to the examination center. It was a stressful time for Risa, and I know I should have been there. I remember Joy scolding me, "One day, Risa will remind you that you chose to go to China for ACTAsia instead of taking her to her first violin examination."

When Risa was seven years old, I had her do extra math homework using an Asian method every evening, not because she was behind in her studies but because I am a tiger mother and wanted her to have every advantage. . . . Again, I was away in China and Joy was with Risa when the nightly ritual of extra math began. Risa was struggling and asked Joy for help. Although Joy could calculate the answers, she was not familiar with the steps of the Asian methodology, which Risa had to enter in her workbook. Joy said, "No problem, Risa, your dad will soon be home; he will help you." But when Ross arrived home, he couldn't figure it out. Risa was getting distressed, so Joy thought to ring her son, who was a teacher. He couldn't do it either. It was then that Risa tearfully said: "I want my mum; she knows how to do it. Can we ring her?" So I received a call from Joy at around 4 a.m. in China, and I spent the next couple of hours on Skype helping Risa with her math homework. It was a trivial matter for an adult, not so for a child.

Yet another time, I was away from home, traveling between Shenzhen and Hong Kong, when Risa was taking part in a school concert, and on more than one occasion, I received distress calls from Risa asking for help with her violin practice. So, bleary-eyed in the early hours of the morning (Hong Kong time), I was coaching Risa for her performance (although I cannot play the violin, I have learned all the theory).

Q13. You have spent your career fighting injustice. What about sexism? What is your personal experience, and what do you think about our progress toward gender equality?

When I was in my teens and early twenties, working with the LCA, I felt like an extension of Wu Hung. When we were together, perhaps attending a meeting or speaking to the media, I often felt like an ornament as the conversation rarely included me, unless I was bold enough to offer a comment or opinion without invitation. One of the reasons I left Taiwan was because I wanted to see what I could do when I was no longer in Wu Hung's or anyone else's shadow, but at the same time, I was fearful that I would be unable to manage on my own.

In China and Taiwan—most Asian countries, in fact—women are seen as inferior to men. When I was growing up, women had no position in society but were expected to do manual work in fields and factories, and every mother wanted a son. Although sex-based prejudice definitely also exists in the West, women in many countries now have access to a stronger platform to demand equality in the workplace and in society. Women and girls need to be brave and speak out if they are being disadvantaged or harassed in educational institutions, in the workplace, or in civic society, but of course, speaking out can be difficult, especially if they feel that their positions, jobs, or reputations could be in jeopardy. This is slowly changing in some Asian countries, but I feel it will take some time yet.

Q14. Who or what has had the most influence on your life?

This is a difficult question for me to answer because I have had many influences in my life, among them certainly Dame Jane Goodall, who inspired me to forge my own path. She is a wonderful example of a single-minded and courageous woman who has made her mark on what once was very much a man's world. Many other people and events have influenced me for different reasons.

Before I left Taiwan, Wu Hung was the most influential person in my life. He and I, a Buddhist monk and his number-one disciple, were seen as a rare combination whenever we traveled together. We worked closely together to fight for justice for voiceless animals. This work, which gave me a way to apply Wu Hung's Buddhist teachings to real life, was a formative experience for my younger self, but I began to wonder if I was just parroting his thoughts and words. This question did eventually motivate me to leave Taiwan: subconsciously, I wanted to find out who I was. Years later, Asir, also a disciple of Wu Hung and an LCA volunteer, told me he thought me brave for having broken the tie with my mentor in order not to become totally dependent.

Yet other influences have come from many of my colleagues in Taiwan and the UK, especially Sarah, Asir, Keda, and Ming Huei, from whom I've learned a lot and whose positive work styles I've tried to emulate. Sharing a happy and loving home with Ross, Risa, and my lovely cat Socks has influenced me to become a more compassionate person. Of course, Buddhism has had a great influence on my ability to rationalize the events of my earlier years so that I no longer feel any anger or bitterness. And throughout the years, meditation has given me a useful channel for reflection after any type of trauma or, conversely, success.

Although my mother had a difficult life, I admire her determination, loyalty, leadership, and hard work; she has influenced me to always persevere in spite of adversity. I wonder how she managed to cope with all the challenges she faced: She was a mistress with little standing in society, five children, a chronically ill partner, and a sharp-tongued mother by adoption. She was practically illiterate and spoke in broken Mandarin. She had had only six years of primary schooling, and for the first four years, she had been taught in the Japanese language, Taiwan being under Japanese rule at that time. When she needed to visit the municipality for family or work registration, one of her children had to act as her interpreter. Despite all these odds, she was a capable woman with an iron determination, who cared for her ill husband, diabetic mother, and five children yet was always neat and tidy. I never saw her cry in despair or self-pity. She never resorted to alcohol or drugs as an escape but just kept forging ahead. From her, I learned the meaning of responsibility and how to find the courage to face challenges in life head-on. She was my best role model.

Q15. When you recall the sexual abuse you experienced as a small girl in Taiwan, have you come to terms with it? What do you think was preventing you from telling your mother or sisters?

I do recall the abuse, but it's almost as if it happened to another person. I still experience feelings of guilt and think it was my fault: In both cases, I wanted to be given the sweets, even though I knew what would be expected of me, and I went back several times. So although I now know the perpetrators, being adults, were guilty of child sexual abuse (a crime), was I just an innocent child or was I knowingly complicit? Why didn't I tell someone what was happening? I wonder if these experiences contributed to my feelings of worthlessness and low self-esteem later on in life. Fortunately, these memories are no longer regularly at the forefront of my mind, although whenever I read of similar cases, the guilt comes back.

In primary school and junior high, I took the bus to school every day with other schoolgirls. We quickly learned we must protect ourselves during the early-morning and after-school crowded bus rides, as men would often seize the opportunity to press their private parts against our backs and move their hands to inappropriately touch us. We did not shout or make a fuss but silently accepted that such behavior just happened and tried to avoid falling victim to it again.

Perhaps partly because of my own experiences, in recent years, I have become greatly intrigued by the cycle of abuse as a subject of study and means of breaking this cycle, and I've read many reports on the links between child abuse or domestic violence and animal abuse. Fortunately, now, unlike in days gone by, victims of abuse are urged to speak out and their voices are amplified, as in the case of the rise of the Me Too movement, a social movement against sexual abuse, harassment, and rape culture. Although there is still some resistance, times are changing.

I don't know why I didn't tell my sisters or my mother about my experiences. (In fact, I didn't tell anyone prior to writing this book.) Perhaps I thought I would get into trouble for taking the sweets? I have no answer. Even now, I find that I am reluctant to think too deeply about what happened to me. Although I understand (in theory) that it is not the fault of a child if they are victimized by a predator, it is hard to overcome feelings of self-blame when it comes to my own experiences. Perhaps some experiences that cannot be changed are best buried in the past. Perhaps this is a cowardly response. I can understand why many victims of abuse remain silent.

Q16. What are your long-term plans for ACTAsia?

The year 2023 marked my thirtieth anniversary working in this movement. There are still few people in Asia doing similar work. Many start, or want to start, but soon get discouraged when faced with the reality of limited political and societal support. Philanthropy without any strings attached is still relatively new in Asia: it is difficult to find support for a cause even from those close to you, such as friends and family.

When I reached the twenty-year mark of my career, I asked myself what I was going to do in the next twenty years. For all my efforts, was the world a better place? I reflected on my work at that time, which consisted mainly of undercover investigations, protests, lobbying for legislative change, and capacity-building strategies for grassroots groups in Asia and elsewhere. I discovered that I had spent much of my time, certainly in the early years, trying to "fix the leaks," taking the "sticking plaster" approach. We were often preaching to the believers and not doing enough to widen our reach to include the non-believers. I vowed to myself that the next twenty years would see us focus on addressing the root causes of social problems through education—hence the birth of our Caring for Life education projects for children, professionals, and consumers.

I also want to work with established institutions such as the United Nations to create change, rather than continue to act as the outsider shouting at anyone who will listen and hoping change will come. I aim to promote our work such that we can reach a wider, global audience and convince decision-makers that the sustainability of our species' future depends on how we care for and respect other animals and nature. Currently, ACTAsia is a member of five United Nations alliances, having passed their rigorous selection processes, and is able to participate in meetings and seminars such as the United Nations High-Level Political Forum on Sustainable Development.

At the outset, I could never have imagined that I would journey from being a somewhat rebellious protestor to being a mainstream educator and wanting to create change from within established global institutions. However, my long-term goal for the future has not changed; with each passing year in my battle for compassion, I just become more focused on the process.

Q17. How are you different now compared to the confused twenty-eight-year-old who left Taiwan?

I am now in a unique and fortunate position, with experience working for social and policy change at both grassroots and international levels, as well as in-depth knowledge of China in particular. I can assess many issues and situations, offering informed thoughts and opinions. In many ways, I have become more tolerant and flexible in my thinking and behavior. I think I am more open, less sensitive to points of view different from my own, and more acclimated to a

Western way of life. I now even eat apple pies, cheese sandwiches, and jacket potatoes—foods that I struggled with for several years. I still feel Asian and have missed not being able to go back to Taiwan during the two years of the COVID-19 pandemic. But I am no longer angry and confused; I have the confidence to strive for my goal in life, which is to lead a successful organization promoting care and respect for all forms of life. Although I am fifty-six, I still aspire to at some point complete a PhD on child development and Caring for Life education, mainly for personal reasons (to prove to myself that I have the ability) but also to create an academic work that others may build on.

I was brought up to work hard. I enjoy working long hours, often at unsociable times, and have always expected those working with me to do likewise. Recently, I've begun to understand that the people I used to think of as lazy are not lazy—they simply choose to prioritize balance between their work life and home life more than I do. Getting the right balance is something I need to work on. But in general, life is good, and I am happy. I've evolved from a young adult who was tired of life with all its struggles to a middle-aged person who is secure in her work life and home life, surrounded by love. The title I have chosen for my book, *Life of Pei: The Battle for Compassion*, has a double meaning: my work with ACTAsia promotes a compassionate world; at the same time, my self-work is an ongoing personal battle for compassion, for myself and others.

I don't recall the words "compassion" and "empathy" ever being used or even having any meaning in Taiwan in my youth. As I was growing up, I felt little concern for those suffering from wars, famine, or poverty elsewhere in the world. Natural calamities like earthquakes and typhoons were a part of life in Taiwan, and war was an ever-present possibility. I was concerned only with the disasters that could befall us and whether we had enough to eat. And when death and loss became a part of my life, I continued to care only about how I was affected and what would happen to me; if I had any compassion, it was for myself. I realize now that I was a rather cold, unfeeling child, teenager, and young adult.

In earnest, I do now feel compassion for my family, friends, and colleagues, as well as for all suffering people in the world. Compassion is a skill that evolves as one finds inner happiness and peace and learns to identify with others. But knowing the definition of compassion is not enough; one needs to take action. ACTAsia and its educational work are how I act on compassion and try to encourage others to do the same. I barely recognize young Pei; it's been a long, hard road of learning about life and about myself, and I hope I have many more years of learning left on this earth before I travel to the next world.

Q18. The industrial farming industry is said to be one of the main contributors to global warming. What is ACTAsia's considered opinion?

Recently, a United Nations report stated that the amount of dairy and meat that people are consuming is fueling global warming. Although research findings vary, it is generally thought that cows, sheep, and goats are responsible for a significant percentage of all greenhouse gases. Since ACTAsia's beginnings, I have been keen on addressing industrialized farming practices, as countless investigations have exposed the misery and suffering billions of animals have to endure to feed and clothe humans. The inhumane conditions these animals are kept in not only compromise their welfare but also cause environmental pollution and threaten human health.

However, it is difficult to address farming issues in China at the present time: the animal protection movement is in its infancy, and ignorance is widespread in the industry as well as among the public. When we visited schools to introduce Caring for Life education, teachers told us that lessons could not include dog eating or vegetarianism/veganism—sensitive topics for Chinese people. If we tried to discourage meat consumption, parents would complain and the authorities would cancel any CFL lessons in their schools. So to avoid potential problems, I decided we would campaign against the fur farming industry as the issue was not as sensitive and the time was right.

I do think that what we eat influences our attitudes, and that abstaining from animal products is an extension of our compassion for all living beings and ourselves, in line with ACTAsia's mission. It is only logical that many people in the animal welfare movement are either vegetarian or vegan. ACTAsia would like to promote a plant-based diet and reduced consumption of animal products, but we must be subtle in our approach. Rather than take huge risks with a direct public campaign, we need to prepare the ground first for mass dietary change—slowly, step by step.

Many Western organizations believe that providing more plant-based food choices—by creating more tofu recipes and investing more in plant-based proteins or cultured meat—is enough to influence attitudes toward meat and create dietary change. But why should people bother changing their diet? What would motivate them to change? They may try eating plant-based for a short while but then slip back into their old ways. As with New Year's resolutions such as giving up alcohol or going on a diet to lose weight, the initial intention is good, but the effort is usually short-lived.

Plant-based proteins and plant-based options are often just business incentives; they are not designed to change hearts and minds. Change requires education, so that consumers are aware that animals are sentient beings. Change requires investment of time, so that people are allowed to learn about the suffering behind the animal farming industry and its implications for the planet. Once convinced of the facts, they may gradually come to accept a new lifestyle. They need to understand why they should change. Yet, the majority of funding opportunities are oriented toward the Western push for plant-based food. I often ask myself in frustration, "Why are my thirty years of observations and suggestions not appreciated or considered?"

Recently, ACTAsia set up an alliance across six countries, called the Compassionate Choices Network (CCN). Through our Plant Forward events, CCN is providing education to help consumers understand the ease of making compassionate dietary choices as well as the benefits—for themselves and for all who share the planet. Our sustainable future is with plants.

Q19. On balance, do you think that all of your work and sacrifices for ACTAsia have been worth it?

YES! As I have mentioned, my years working for social change and with ACTAsia have presented me with challenges and opportunities that I could never have anticipated in my wilderness days, one of the biggest challenges being our current reliance on mass digital media, which makes effective communication difficult without costly professional technical input. Nevertheless, my work has enabled me to grow as a person and develop a sense of self-worth, giving me the confidence to strive for a kinder world for people, animals, and the environment. Like most people, I still have days when feelings of disappointment and self-doubt take over, but I can now shake off those feelings and stay in control of my life.

I hope that by reading about my story and my journey from this book, you will understand what I am trying to do. I hope you will feel motivated to join me and ACTAsia in the battle for compassion. Together, we can make our world a kinder and more compassionate one for its inhabitants, human and nonhuman, and the environment, all the while remembering that we are all interconnected in this wonderful web of life.

My journey along my chosen path continues.
ACTAsia's mission through education continues.
My battle for compassion continues.

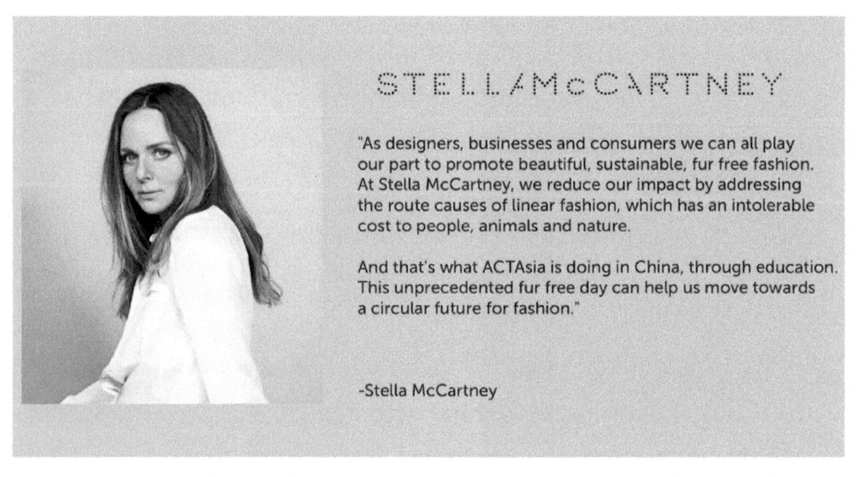

2020. Support from the world-renowned fashion house, Stella McCartney, for the ACTAsia Fur Free Fashion Show in Shanghai.

Afterword

In February 2023, my stable, comfortable world suddenly came crashing down when I heard these four words, "you have breast cancer." The doctor continued talking, but I was not hearing his words. Then his next sentence caught my attention, "It's at an early stage but the tests show you have a Grade 3 aggressive fast-growing tumor." This revelation seemed to pierce my brain as if I had been stabbed. In a state of shock, I felt as if I was being transported to another planet, as this was the closest, I had ever felt to having an out-of-body experience.

A few months before, in October 2022, I became aware of a slight discomfort in my chest, especially when in bed and turning onto my side. But could I feel a small lump? I wasn't sure, probably my imagination. I shrugged it off thinking perhaps I had pulled a muscle or bruised a rib during exercise, but after a few weeks, the niggling discomfort was still no better, so I made an appointment to see my doctor. The doctor's surgery was busy with patients suffering from colds and respiratory infections, as is usual in the UK during the winter months, so thinking I didn't need an urgent appointment, I accepted an appointment for 9 January 2023.

At my appointment when examining me, my doctor could also feel a small lump but was not unduly concerned, suggesting it could be a cyst, which commonly occurs in women of menopausal age. But to be sure, she advised I should have a mammogram. The scan clearly revealed an abnormal lump that needed further investigation, so the next step was to have a biopsy. Although when originally discovering the lump, I was fully aware that it may not be a cyst, I somehow blanked out of my mind the possibility of it being a cancerous tumor. But as the result of the biopsy unfolded, the word cancer seemed to reverberate around the room and was the only word that registered in my brain.

As I heard more of the diagnosis and treatment, I could almost feel my heart falling through my torso and plunging deep into the ground. I couldn't breathe, I couldn't speak. Time came to a halt as I screamed in silence, my seemingly frozen body numbing all my senses. My horror and disbelief quickly turned to anger and self-pity.

I have no time for illness, I'm much too busy with ACTAsia. Why me? What have I done to deserve this? Haven't I suffered enough in my life?

Suddenly, my brain switched back to reality as my thoughts focused on my daughter Risa and visions of my demise started to race through my mind.

Oh no, this cannot be happening, I cannot die, my daughter is only sixteen. Is history repeating itself?

My thoughts traveled back to the time when my mother died, when I was a similar age to Risa. I started to relive in my mind the despair and agony I felt when losing my beloved Mum, the long-lasting raw pain that followed and how in my despair I spiralled out of control.

I must not let something similar happen to Risa, especially at a time when she is so close to taking important school exams, which will influence her future. I must win the battle I am being forced to confront.

Being a Tiger Mother, even before the day Risa was born, I aimed to provide a stable home for her and ensure that she grew into a diligent student who would go on to study at a prestigious university, such as Oxford, and have every chance to achieve her potential. So, it was essential that I could not allow her to see me in despair at this crucial time in her life. She must not have the worry and the burden of a dying mother. I must not allow her to become overwhelmed with uncertainty to such an extent that her studies may be pushed into the background, perhaps even become irrelevant.

Once I came to terms with my situation, I knew I had to find a way to manage this challenge as it could not be avoided or swept away into the background. Many people advised me to forget about ACTAsia and focus on getting well, letting others carry the burden. But, stubborn as always, I was determined to try and work whilst following the necessary treatment plan.

The plan was made up of several months of treatment; chemotherapy to shrink the tumor; an operation to remove the tumor, and to remove a wide margin of surrounding tissue; radiotherapy; target therapy; followed by five years of hormone treatment. My family and friends in Taiwan were distraught to learn that I would not be going back to my native homeland to have the treatment. "But you must," wailed my sisters, "we want to look after you, we are so worried about you." I replied, "My home is here with Ross and Risa, they need me with them, and I need to stay close to them." Reluctantly my Taiwan family knew that I could not be swayed.

I realized how little I knew about cancer, its treatment, and its side effects. I started to search through numerous internet sites and was amazed to find that one in two people will develop some form of cancer during their lifetime, with breast cancer being the most diagnosed type of cancer. Fortunately, I have two long-term friends who are experienced hospital doctors: Dr. Helen Winter, a Consultant Medical Oncologist, and Dr. Simmie Manchandra, a Consultant Physician. From my diagnosis to the present time, they have been able to help and advise me and above all explain in simple terminology what I was likely to encounter on the rocky path of my treatment plan, through to recovery. I am fully aware that although fate has been unkind to me, I am indeed blessed to receive the ongoing care and kindness from these two busy professionals. Likewise, my hospital oncology team has guided me and will continue to guide me through the coming months and years.

The day I started chemotherapy, I was largely stepping into the unknown, even though I had been reading medical journals and articles about cancer, treatments, and possible outcomes for the previous few weeks. All I knew for certain at this stage was that the coming months were likely to be fraught with anxiety and discomfort. I knew that chemotherapy is used to target a wide range of cancers, but also knew that the chemicals in the chemotherapy medication that destroy cancerous cells can also damage healthy cells, leading to common side effects such as hair loss, nausea, tiredness, and anaemia, to name just a few. But it was not possible to predict how my body would react to the treatment, as patients differ one from another, so I clung to the fact that not every cancer patient is plagued with side effects and even if I did get any, they may not be too severe. So, although somewhat apprehensive, I was relatively upbeat and tried to be positive, determined to overcome this unwelcome challenge.

On hearing that I had cancer, Clare, and Debbie, two friends in my village formed a small help group and organized the group to prepare all meals for Ross, Risa, and me throughout the long weeks and months of my treatment and hospitalization. They continue to make sure I am regularly taken out for short walks, for treats such as visits to a coffee shop, or simply a car drive to an area of natural beauty and they encourage me to celebrate every small milestone. Friends who work full-time take me out on Saturdays or Sundays, even though their own time is limited. Such a wonderful show of care and concern from local people in my village continues to move me and helps me to evaluate the life I've been given. One of ACTAsia's well-used quotes, *compassion in action*, is demonstrated every day by my caring village friends. They are like a family to me, so the fears of my family in Taiwan thinking I would have no one to care for me, are unfounded.

It now seems ironic that when I moved to this village I felt like an alien, I made no friends for several years and felt inferior, an outsider, yet now I need help more than at any time since arriving in the UK, they are caring for me as one of their own. I certainly did not envisage such kindness and compassion from people I hardly knew before my illness, especially as the British culture is often labelled as rather cold and distant. But now I feel at home in the UK and at last have a sense of belonging and greatly appreciate the type of kindness and friendship that I knew so well in my own country.

My first visit to the hospital for chemotherapy passed without any significant trauma. I attended a relatively small hospital in a nearby town, where the nurses were all warm and kind, yet businesslike and radiated confidence. The first dose of chemotherapy was given via an intravenous drip inserted into my arm and took about two hours to complete. During this time, I was able to use the room as my office and get on with some ACTAsia work, much to the intrigue of the nurses who were not used to having an energetic, workaholic patient, determined to focus on her work, cancer, or no cancer.

The next day I started to feel nauseous, tired, and cold, and for the following couple of days, I felt increasingly worse. Within days I noticed when brushing my hair, there were long strands of black hair clinging to my hairbrush. I knew the chemotherapy was causing my hair to drop out, and it was a very scary experience. I loved having long hair but to help Risa and myself get over the shock of unavoidable hair loss, I decided we would go together to the hairdresser, and Risa could see me have my hair cut short, so within a few days this happened. But only a week or so later, I had a vivid dream where I found lots of hair on my pillow and bald patches were appearing all over my head. This dream had a profound effect on me, and I realized that knowing I would lose all my hair, was increasing my anxiety levels. Rather than face the stress of finding lumps of fallen hair and bald patches as in my dream, it was time to be proactive, so collectively Ross, Risa, and I shaved off my thinning hair.

2023. Losing my hair to chemotherapy.

Losing one's hair is a dramatic occurrence for women, but for me, having lived among female monks in Taiwan where it is customary for them to have shaved heads, and having trained to be a monk and accepted that I would also have a shaved head, it had never unduly concerned me. But now years later living a different lifestyle, with a different way of thinking, I understand that what might be seen as vanity, is part of one's identity. I now wear a small hat indoors that warmly encloses my bare head, plus a range of glamorous wigs when venturing outside of my home.

Each three-weekly chemotherapy cycle was followed by a swarm of side effects, becoming increasingly worse after each cycle. Each time the side effects would last for more than a week; nausea, painful headaches, fatigue, aching body, and brain fog were the main symptoms. I rapidly became very ill and developed neutropenic sepsis on several occasions, a potentially life-threatening condition. On each occasion, I was admitted to the hospital, where I stayed in isolation for seven to ten days.

These were some of my darkest days and I prayed to every god in the universe to have mercy on my soul and spare me, as I needed to recover and look after my child. Ross coped well with this crisis period and was much calmer than I expected, sometimes almost appearing detached, but always positive about the eventual outcome. Yet Risa has a more complex personality, and her slender frame dropped more weight as she agonized over her looming exams and my weakening condition. I knew she was fearful during this period and when I returned home from the hospital, I vowed to put on an act to convince her I was recovering.

She had seen a magazine article that recommended exercise to help prevent metastasis, so she would often say, "Please Mum, go and do some exercise." In response, I did some mild exercise when able to muster the energy as I felt I must show her in action, rather than in words, that I was not sick and dying. Even when feeling extremely fatigued and barely able to drag my body along, I sit down as much as I can, so she is not aware of my weak, trembling legs and I do not stay in bed when she is at home. Above all, I make sure I give her a meal every evening (prepared by the village ladies) and sit with her while she eats it. I smile as I realize that I am behaving just as my mother did all those years ago, when her priority, above all else, was to feed us a nourishing meal and project an impression that all was well—there was nothing to worry about—her way of showing her love for us.

The sixteen cycles of chemotherapy were so challenging, with most, if not all, of the side effects listed in medical textbooks, visiting me at one time or another. A further stay in hospital for ten days yet again with neutropenic sepsis, dragged me down both physically and mentally and my Hospital Consultant decided that he would not be giving me the final two scheduled cycles of the chemotherapy plan, as my general condition was so weak.

About one month later, an MRI scan (magnetic resonance imaging scan) showed that the chemotherapy treatment had caused the tumor to shrink, and it could now be removed, so I returned to the hospital for a lumpectomy operation. It went ahead smoothly, and the surgeon told me he had removed what was left of the tumor. All that was needed now was a course of radiotherapy to blast any fragments that might be lurking undetected. I was so happy as the side effects of the chemotherapy were now fading and I was starting to feel much better. Also, the ACTAsia staff and volunteers in China and the UK, had learned to take on more responsibility during the lockdown period of COVID-19, so were now able to make decisions in my absence. This was a great relief for me and took away unnecessary pressure as I started to plan how I would ease myself back into full-time work.

A week later I had a scheduled appointment with my Oncologist, to find out when the radiotherapy sessions would begin. I was not prepared for the shock I was about to encounter. In disbelief, once again I experienced the old familiar numb feeling sweep over me, as I heard him say, "The biopsy we took at the operation showed you still have some residual cancer cells." *What?* I wanted to scream and scream and scream, *this cannot be happening, I have just completed eight months of grueling treatment.* I could vaguely hear him saying, "You now have a choice, you can either continue with our original plan or you can have a relatively new type of treatment to make sure we kill off any rogue cells. It combines target antibody drugs with chemotherapy. This would be twelve cycles over nine months."

I was so shocked and upset as I thought I had come through the difficult and painful treatment and in the future would just have to take hormone tablets.

"What do you mean, a choice" was my response, "there is no choice, I have a sixteen-year-old daughter. I have to survive and if that means more treatment, then I must have it." I cried uncontrollably when thinking of a further nine months of aggressive treatment and the potential side effects, although I knew I must have the treatment.

The first cycle blasted my system and the all too familiar side effects immediately sent me on a downward spiral, so yet again I was back in hospital with a life-threatening infection.

At the time of writing this Afterword, I have been taken off treatment as my body at this stage cannot cope too well, but I will shortly begin a less aggressive, more targeted treatment. So, what has this cruel and inconvenient disease taught me? I thought when writing the main body of this book I had grown to know myself and my life was under control. But going through the experience of cancer, with all the fears and doubts that accompany each stage of the disease, it seems only logical that my mindset has changed from my pre-cancer days. My priorities in the past, in this order, were ACTAsia's work, finding the funds to enable more work, finding enough staff and volunteers to do the work, family, home, friends, and then me.

This is a long list, so the priorities at the lower end of the list were often forgotten. I was always in work mode. Even when on family holidays I struggled to switch off. But the shock of a cancer diagnosis with the side effects of chemotherapy, and the fear of death, is a great leveller. The order of one's priorities rapidly shifts, and I was forced to go into survival mode. I have recently learned to think differently about myself and others. I feel very grateful to be looked after with such care and consideration and to have so many compassionate friends.

My life-changing experiences are teaching me the true meaning of empathy and compassion. Before my cancer diagnosis, I thought I clearly understood the meaning of this terminology but having personally experienced empathy and compassion from others when at my lowest ebb, it now holds deeper meaning for me. The words of Sir William Osler ring loud in my ears (as referenced in Chapter 12) when he infers that care, compassion, and kindness are equally as important to a patient's mindset and recovery as conventional medication, perhaps even more so when a patient is terminally ill and fearful of their impending demise.

I find it boring to be ill, especially when too ill to concentrate on reading a book or watching TV. But at such times the radio is just about tolerable. It was on one such occasion that I discovered the work of Dr. Gabor Mate, a Canadian Physician. In his book, titled: *When the Body Says No: The Cost of Hidden Stress,* he states:

Emotional stress is a major cause of physical illness, from cancer to autoimmune conditions and many other chronic diseases. The brain and body systems that process emotions are intimately connected with the hormonal apparatus, the nervous system, and particularly the immune system.

Did I bring my illness on by pushing myself too hard, neglecting regular meals and sleep, and ignoring burn-out warnings from my friends? Dr. Gabor's book made me realize that although I promote compassion and empathy for animals, other humans, and the environment, I have overlooked being compassionate towards myself. Have I ignored my body's physical needs to the point where I have developed cancer, and this is my body's way of saying No to me?

I am no longer angry with my cancer and somewhat perversely, I have learned to appreciate it. Why? Because without this cruel disease, I would probably never have stopped working at such a demonic pace, regardless of other warnings. I liken myself to a juvenile offender who is fortunate enough to be given a second chance to reflect on his thoughtless wrongdoing, which has hurt himself and others. I know now more than at any time before, that the battle for compassion lies within me.

I still have at least another nine months of treatment ahead of me and there is no guarantee that I will ultimately win the battle.

Still, I am confident that with the wonderful continuing support from family, friends, and the medical team, I have more than a fighting chance of a full recovery. I will persevere with my cancer treatment, even though at times the side effects drain my resolve. But so many people during this past year have reminded me that I am a strong woman, one person even said, "Perseverance has another name, it's called Pei."

I will conclude this book by naming the wonderful people who are beside me as I travel through my cancer experience. They make the reality so much easier to bear. Their care and compassion will be remembered by me for the rest of my days. My family and I are truly grateful.

Doctors at Chiltern Hospital: Giles Cunnick; Allan Makepeace.

Oncology Nurses at Chiltern Hospital: Catherine; Emilia; Hilary; Haley, Loredana; Rebecca; Sandra.

Friends in Penn Village: Jasmine Badcock; Zeynep Bezer; Jo Dawtrey; Sam & Sura Elias; Catherine Jimenez; Aurelie Johnson; Jackie Lambert; Clare Shearston; Michelle South; Debbie Workmen; Vibha Verma; Wai Wong.

Family and friends in Taiwan, UK & many other countries, especially: My sisters, Kim Bartlett; Fion Berriman; Hui-Chaun Chen; Holly Dyer; Vadivu Govind; Joy Leney; Dr. Simmie Manchandra; Dave McCourt; Aashi Patel; Veda Stram; Vivian Trundley; Sally Tsai; Dr. Helen Winter; Sarah Wu; Brenda Young; Yu Min-Chen; Yue -Xin Lee.

ACTAsia Board Members, staff & supporters.

Bibliography and References

Preface

- United Nations Development Program Annual Report 2022. *Sustainable Development Goals 2030.* New York City: United Nations, 2023.
- Kuomintang (KMT). *History 1894 - 2006.* Official Website of the KMT, Taipei, Taiwan. 2023. http://www1.kmt.org.tw/.

Chapter 1

- Juagdan, Alexie. *Filial Piety in Chinese Culture: A Timeless Tradition.* Asian Journal USA. 14 August 2023. www.asianjournalusa.com.
- Harrison, Mark. *The End of Martial Law: An Important Anniversary for Taiwan.* Global Taiwan Institute. Vol.2, issue 30. 26 July 2017. https://globaltaiwan.org.
- Leney, Nick and ACTAsia. *Caring for Life Education Curriculum Framework & Guidelines.* ACTAsia for Animals. 2014. Updated 2021. www.actasia.org/resources.
- Leney, Nick and ACTAsia. *Caring for Life Education Standard.* ACTAsia for Animals. 2014. Updated 2021. www.actasia.org/resources.
- Attributed to Stephen Hawking. Hawking, Stephen and Leonard Mlodinow. *The Grand Design.* New York: Bantam Books, 2010.

Chapter 2

- Wakeman, Frederic Jr. *Spymaster: Dai Li and the Chinese Secret Service.* Berkeley and Los Angeles: University of California Press, 2003.

Chapter 3

- BBC News. *Explainer: What was China's One-Child Policy?* BBC NEWS China. 29 October 2015. www.bbc.co.uk/news/world-asia-china-34667551.

- Cartwright, Mark. *Foot Binding.* World History Encyclopedia. Last modified 27 September 2017. https://www.worldhistory.org/Foot-Binding/.

Chapter 4

- McEneaney, Ciaran. *A Brief History of Ghost Month.* Culture Trip Guide. 31 March 2018. https://theculturetrip.com/asia/Taiwan/articles/a-brief-history-of-ghost-month.
- Wang Yu Wei and Heppner PP. *A Qualitative Study of Childhood Sexual Abuse Survivors in Taiwan: Toward a Transactional and Ecological Model of Coping.* J Couns Psychol. 58(3):393-409. doi: 10.1037/a0023522. PMID: 21574695. July 2011.
- Too, Lillian. *The Complete Illustrated Guide to Feng Shui.* London: Element. 2002.

Chapter 6

- Bonner, John. *Taiwan's Tragic Orang-Utans.* New Scientist. 3 December 1994. https://www.newscientist.com/article/mg14419541-400.
- Pires, Stephen F., and William D. Moreto. *The Illegal Wildlife Trade: Oxford Handbook Topics in Criminology and Criminal Justice.* Oxford: Oxford University Press. online edition 2012, Oxford Academic, 2 June 2014. https://doi.org/10.1093/oxfordhb/9780199935383.013.161.

Chapter 7

- UK Government Farm Animal Welfare Council. *The Five Freedoms of Animal Welfare.* London: Farm Animal Welfare Council. 1979.
- Leney, Joy, and Marks, David. *Disposable Dogs: Made in Taiwan.* The World Society for the Protection of Animals (now known as World Animal Protection). 1995. https://worldanimalprotection.org.

Chapter 9

- World Health Organization and The World Society for the Protection of Animals. *The Management & Control of Stray & Unwanted Animals.* Geneva: World Health Organization. 1993.

Chapter 10

- Bhiksu, Wu Hung; Phillips, Tim; Wilson Phillip. *The Global Trade in Bear Products from China to Asia & Beyond.* London: The World Society for the Protection of Animals. 2002.

Chapter 11

- Hsieh-Yi; Yi-Chiao; Yu Fu; (EAST); Maas, Barbara, (Care for the Wild); Rissi, Mark, (Swiss Animal Protection). *Dying for Fur: A Report on the Fur Industry in China.* Zurich: Swiss Animal Protection. 2005. Updated 25 January 2007.
- ACTAsia. *Report of Dog and Cat Fur Trade in China.* ACTAsia. 2017. www.actasia.org/resources.
- Kotuwage, Dawn and Cecilia Fischer. *China's Fur Trade and its Position in the Global Fur Industry. Update Executive Summary 2020/2021.* ACTAsia. June 2022. https://actasia.org/ACTAsia-Chinas-Fur-Industry-report-2022-Executive -Summary-1.pdf.
- Leney, Joy. *Such a Nuisance to Die: The Autobiography of Her Serene Highness Princess Elisabeth de Croÿ.* Brighton: Book Guild Publishing. 2010.
- Balaram, Deepashree and Su, Pei F. *Changing China: Country status report within the political and social context.* ACTAsia for Animals. 2011. www.actasia.org/resources.

Chapter 12

- Samuels, William Ellery. *Caring for Life Education: Evaluation Results 2013-2016.* ACTAsia. 26 November 2017. www.actasia.org/resources.
- Sudworth, John. *Counting the cost of China's left-behind children.* BBC NEWS China. 12 April 2016. https://www.bbc.co.uk/news/world-asia-china-35994481.
- Cranston, David. *William Osler and his Legacy to Medicine.* Bicester: Words by Design. 2017.

Chapter 13

- ACTAsia and FurFree Alliance. *Toxic Fur: A Global Issue, Research in China.* ACTAsia. 21 November 2018. www.actasia.org/resources.

- Phillips, Allie. *Understanding the Link between Violence to Animals and People: A Guidebook for Criminal Justice Professionals.* Arlington, USA: National District Attorneys Association. 2014.
- Zinsstag, Jakob et al. *One Health: The Theory and Practice of Integrated Health.* Wallingford: CABI Publishing, 2nd Edition 2 November 2020.

Chapter 14

- Sato, Shozo. Ikebana: The Art of Arranging Flowers. North Clarendon, Vermont: Tuttle Shokai inc. Reprint edition 22 April 2013.

Photographs and Credits

Pei Su holds the copyright for all photographs used in *Life of Pei*, except the following:

- Cover photo: 2022. Pei-Feng Su. Credit: You-Wei Chen. Taipei.
- Page 66. 1995. Polar bear in Taipei Zoo with skin infection. Credit: Life Conservationist Association of Taiwan.
- Page 234. 2020. Support from the world-renowned fashion house, Stella McCartney, for the ACTAsia Fur Free Fashion Show in Shanghai. Credit: Stella McCartney Ltd.

Organizations

- ACTAsia Head Office. PO Box 1264 High Wycombe. HP10 8WL. UK, incorporating AsiaLink and Institute for Caring for Life Academic Research and Education (iCARE): https://www.actasia.org
- American Humane Society, USA: https://www.americanhumane.org
- American Society for the Prevention of Cruelty to Animals (ASPCA): https://www.aspca.org
- Animal Welfare Institute (AWI): https://www.awionline.org
- Animals Asia: https://www.animalsasia.org
- Animals for Asia Coalition (AFA): https://www.asiaforanimals.com
- Boxhill Veterinary Clinic: https://www.balwyncentralvet.com.au
- British Broadcasting Corporation (BBC): https://www.bbc.com
- British Sky Broadcasting (Sky UK): https://www.sky.com
- Cable News Network (CNN): https://www.cnn.com
- Care for the Wild: https://www.careforthewild.org
- China Biodiversity Conservation & Green Development Foundation: https://www.cbcgdf.org
- Defense et Protection des Animaux (DPA) Refuge de Thiernay: https://www.refuge-thiernay.com
- Deutsche Welle: https://www.dw.com
- Dogs Trust: https://www.dogstrust.org.uk
- EndPandemics: https://www.endpandemics.earth
- Environment & Animal Society of Taiwan (EAST): https://www.east.org.tw
- Environmental Investigation Agency (EIA): https://eia-international.org
- Farm Sanctuary: https://www.farmsanctuary.org
- Four Paws: https://www.four-paws.org.uk
- Geneva Animal Protection Society: https://www.animal-protection.net
- Global Alliance for Rabies Control: https://www.rabiesalliance.org
- Green Chimneys: https://www.greenchimneys.org
- Help in Suffering (HIS): https://www.helpinsuffering.org

- Humane Society of the United States of America (HSUS): https://www.humanesociety.org
- Humane Society International (HSI): https://www.hsi.org
- Institute for Humane Education: https://humaneeducation.org
- International Association of Human-Animals Interaction Organisations (IAHAIO): https://www.iahaio.org
- International Cat Care: https://www.icatcare.org
- International Society of Animal Rights: https://www.isaronline.org
- Jane Goodall's Roots & Shoots: https://www.rootsnshoots.org.uk
- Legislative Yuan (Parliament): https://www.ly.gov.tw
- Life Conservationist Association (LCA): https://www.lcatwn@ms15.hinet.net
- Massachusetts Society for the Prevention of Cruelty to Animals (MSPCA): https://www.mspca.org
- Naturewatch Foundation: https://www.naturewatch.org
- Osler-McGovern Center, Green Templeton University, Oxford: https://www.gtc.ox.ac.uk
- People's Ethical Treatment of Animals (PETA): https://www.peta.org
- Royal Society for the Prevention of Cruelty to Animals (RSPCA): https://www.rspca.org.uk
- Swiss Animal Protection (SAP): https://www.animal-protection.net
- The Turtle Conservancy: https://www.turtleconservancy.org
- United Nations Economic & Social Council (ECOSOC): https://www.un.org/ecosoc
- University of Kent Colchester Campus: https://www.essex.ac.uk
- University of London College of Fashion (UCL CF): https://www.arts.ac.uk/colleges/london-college-of-fashion
- Vets for Compassion (VFC): https://www.vetsforcompassion.org
- Vogue Business Fashion Industry: https://www.voguebusiness.com
- World Animal Net (WAN): https://www.worldanimal.net
- World Animal Protection (WAP): https://www.worldanimalprotection.org.uk
- World Health Organisation: https://www.who.int

- World Small Animal Veterinary Association (WSAVA): https://www.wsava.org
- World Society for the Protection of Animals (WSPA). Now re-named as World Animal Protection: https://www.worldanimalprotection.org.uk
- Zoocheck Canada: https://www.zoocheck.com
- Zurich Animal Protection Society: https://www.angloinfo.com

The Location of China in Asia

The Reach of ACTAsia in China

A. Beijing City
B. Fujian Province
C. Gansu Province
D. Guangdong Province
E. Guangxi Zhuang Autonomous Region
F. Guizhou Province
G. Hainan Province
H. Hebei Province
I. Heilongjiang Province
J. Henan Province
K. Hubei Province
L. Hunan Province
M. Jiangsu Province
N. Jiangxi Province
O. Jilin Province
P. Shaanxi Province
Q. Shanghai City
R. Shanxi Province
S. Sichuan Province
T. The Inner Mongolia Autonomous Region
U. Tianjin city
V. Tibet Autonomous Region
W. Xinjiang Uygur Autonomous Region
X. Yunnan Province
Y. Zhejiang Province

International Surveys and Covert Investigations 1994–2014

China, Indonesia, Japan, Korea, Malaysia, Myanmar, Singapore, Thailand
International trade in bear bile & other body parts, used in TCM.

China & Taiwan
The illegal wildlife trade in rhino horn, ivory, tiger bone, bear bile & parts, snakes, orangutans.

Australia, Canada, Netherlands, New Zealand, USA
International trade in bear bile & other body pards, used in TCM.

Taiwan
Factory farming & live animal markets.

China & Korea
Dog & cat meat trade for human consumption.

Japan
Bears in entertainment parks.

Indonesia
Animals for entertainment in zoos & circuses.

Hong Kong, Japan, Korea, Taiwan.
International pedigree dog trade.

Taiwan
Government stray dog facilities & dog meat industry.

China & Korea
Bears farms.

Bali
Sea turtle trade.

China
Fur farming; dog & cat fur trade.

Bali & Japan
Hawksbill turtle trade from Bali to Japan.

About the Author

Pei Su founded ACTAsia, a charitable organization, in 2006 to promote kindness and compassion through educational initiatives in Asia. Her background was one of hardships: the deaths of her parents, grandmother, and other close family members by the time she was only 16, had a significant impact on her thinking and behavior, taking her on a path of self-destruction. Eventually, mainly through studying Buddhism and the influence of her Buddhist friends, she overcame many challenges and decided to travel to the UK, where she successfully completed an MA in Sociology Policy. On completing her studies, she found employment with the World Society for the Protection of Animals as Director for Member Societies, leaving after five years to establish ACTAsia. Pei is an international presenter at conferences and in the media, a visiting lecturer at the University of London College of Fashion and Suzhou University, in Shanghai.

About the Publisher

Lantern Publishing & Media was founded in 2020 to follow and expand on the legacy of Lantern Books—a publishing company started in 1999 on the principles of living with a greater depth and commitment to the preservation of the natural world. Like its predecessor, Lantern Publishing & Media produces books on animal advocacy, veganism, religion, social justice, humane education, psychology, family therapy, and recovery. Lantern is dedicated to printing in the United States on recycled paper and saving resources in our day-to-day operations. Our titles are also available as ebooks and audiobooks.

To catch up on Lantern's publishing program, visit us at www.lanternpm.org.

facebook.com/lanternpm
twitter.com/lanternpm
instagram.com/lanternpm